Cambridge Elements

Elements in Translation and Interpreting
edited by
Kirsten Malmkjær
University of Leicester

HYPERTRANSLATION

Mª Carmen África Vidal Claramonte
University of Salamanca

Tong King Lee
University of Hong Kong

CAMBRIDGE UNIVERSITY PRESS

CAMBRIDGE
UNIVERSITY PRESS

Shaftesbury Road, Cambridge CB2 8EA, United Kingdom

One Liberty Plaza, 20th Floor, New York, NY 10006, USA

477 Williamstown Road, Port Melbourne, VIC 3207, Australia

314–321, 3rd Floor, Plot 3, Splendor Forum, Jasola District Centre, New Delhi – 110025, India

103 Penang Road, #05–06/07, Visioncrest Commercial, Singapore 238467

Cambridge University Press is part of Cambridge University Press & Assessment, a department of the University of Cambridge.

We share the University's mission to contribute to society through the pursuit of education, learning and research at the highest international levels of excellence.

www.cambridge.org
Information on this title: www.cambridge.org/9781009518802

DOI: 10.1017/9781009518826

© Mª Carmen África Vidal Claramonte and Tong King Lee 2024

This publication is in copyright. Subject to statutory exception and to the provisions of relevant collective licensing agreements, no reproduction of any part may take place without the written permission of Cambridge University Press & Assessment.

When citing this work, please include a reference to the DOI 10.1017/9781009518826

First published 2024

A catalogue record for this publication is available from the British Library.

ISBN 978-1-009-51880-2 Hardback
ISBN 978-1009-51881-9 Paperback
ISSN 2633-6480 (online)
ISSN 2633-6472 (print)

Cambridge University Press & Assessment has no responsibility for the persistence or accuracy of URLs for external or third-party internet websites referred to in this publication and does not guarantee that any content on such websites is, or will remain, accurate or appropriate.

Hypertranslation

Elements in Translation and Interpreting

DOI: 10.1017/9781009518826
First published online: November 2024

Mª Carmen África Vidal Claramonte
University of Salamanca

Tong King Lee
University of Hong Kong

Author for correspondence: Mª Carmen África Vidal Claramonte, africa@usal.es

Abstract: Hypertranslation refers to a vast and virtual field of mobile relations comprising the interplay of signs across languages, modes, and media. In hypertranslation, the notions of source/target, directionality, and authenticity are set in perpetual flow and flux, resulting in a many-to-many interactive dynamic. Using illustrations drawn from a wide range of literary and artistic experiments, this Element proposes hypertranslation as a theoretical lens on the heterogeneous, remediational, extrapolative, and networked nature of cultural and knowledge production, particularly in cyberspace. It considers how developments in artificial intelligence have led to an expansion in intersemiotic potentialities and the liquidation of imagined boundaries. Exploring the translational aspects of our altered semiotic ecology, where the production, circulation, consumption, and recycling of memes extend beyond human intellect and creativity, this Element positions hypertranslation as a fundamental condition of contemporary posthuman communication in Web 5.0 and beyond.

Keywords: hypertranslation, multimodality, contemporary art, experimental writing, generative artificial intelligence

© Mª Carmen África Vidal Claramonte and Tong King Lee 2024

ISBNs: 9781009518802 (HB), 9781009518819 (PB), 9781009518826 (OC)
ISSNs: 2633-6480 (online), 2633-6472 (print)

Contents

1 Translating Beyond — 1

2 What Is So *Hyper* about Hypertranslation? — 6

3 Hypertranslational Re-readings of Language Art — 21

4 Memes, Intersemioticity, and Experientiality — 31

5 Hyperreality: When the Body Translates — 39

6 Apropos of AI: Hypertranslation as a Semiotic Condition — 47

7 Conclusion — 58

References — 65

1 Translating Beyond

The Japanese best-seller *Nietzsche's Words* 超訳ニーチェの言葉 by Haruhiko Shiratori (2010) popularized the neologism *chōyaku* 超訳, literally 'beyond-translation'; or, better still, to highlight the term's hyperbolism, 'super-translation'. The term was coined by publishers in Japan to describe the making of modern, accessible interpretations of foreign-language texts in the contemporary idiom for the lay audience. A plethora of English terms are available in translation studies to describe relevant phenomena: adaptation, appropriation (Sanders 2016), and whatnot. Still, the popularity of *chōyaku* and its dissemination beyond Japanese discourses offer an opportunity for an excursion in intercultural terminology. In particular, the idea of 'beyond-ness' stokes the paradoxical tension within translation as a limit-concept, with terms like anti-translation, untranslation, dystranslation, mistranslation, counter-translation, and transtranslation coined at one time or another to articulate a 'poetics of opposition and renewal' in translation (Washbourne 2023). Adopting this ethos of translation beyond translating, let us venture to meta-translate the Japanese neologism in English: hypertranslation.

The idea of hypertranslation is not entirely new, though it is, perhaps surprisingly, not quite a term of art in translation studies. A search in the third edition of *Routledge Encyclopedia of Translation Studies* (Baker & Saldanha 2019) yields zero count for the term; nor is it featured in other references such as the *Dictionary of Translation Studies* (Shuttleworth & Cowrie 2014)[1] and *Key Terms in Translation Studies* (Palumbo 2009). In the lesser-known volume *Translation Terminology* (Delisle et al. 1999), hypertranslation does make a brief appearance, only to be dismissed as a 'methodological error' (p. 143) where a translator systematically substitutes a word in the target language for a different word in the source text when a more obvious equivalent is available. In comparative literature, hypertranslation connotes over-interpretation, specifically the 'presenting as part of the text meanings and events that are not there, but whose presence we expect' (Cook 1980: 331). Here hypertranslation is a hermeneutical problem that puts an original text at the risk of being 'traduced', the latter term instantly recalling the age-old, overused maxim *traduttore, traditore* (the translator is a traitor).

It was the philosopher Alain Badiou who popularized hypertranslation, which in *The Communist Hypothesis* describes his adaptive rendition of

---

[1] The term that comes closest is hyperinformation, referring to 'information which is interpolated by the interpreter in order to compensate for the hearer's possible lack of any cultural background knowledge which is necessary for a proper understanding of the message' (Shuttleworth & Currie 2014: 72). Interpolation, it should be noted, is the obverse of hypertranslation, which radically extrapolates a text into virtual, transmodal spaces beyond its constitutive frame.

Plato's *Republic* that came about as part of his 'multifaceted commitment to something like a renaissance of the use of Plato' (Badiou 2010: 230n1). Susan Spitzer, the English-language translator of *Plato's Republic* – Badiou's French rendition of Plato – explains hypertranslation as follows:

> Not a 'simple' translation into French of the Greek original, then, and still less a scholarly critique of it, Badiou's text transforms the *Republic* into something startlingly new by expanding, reducing, updating and dramatizing, leavening it with humour and revitalizing its language with his own philosophical lexicon. Yet, for all the plasticity of the hypertranslation, its free-wheeling appropriation of the source text, it still remains an adaptation based firmly on his painstaking translation of Plato's language into modern French ... Such a hypertranslation inevitably problematizes the task of the translator, who must not lose sight of Plato's *Republic* even as it undergoes myriad transformations in its new French incarnation. (Spitzer 2012: xxiv)

Coming into focus here is the paradoxical tension between Badiou's 'freewheeling appropriation' and 'painstaking translation' of Plato's language arising from two concurrent and contradictory impulses: one centrifugal ('expanding, reducing, updating, dramatizing', etc.) and the other centripetal ('must not lose sight of Plato's *Republic*'). It is this tension that constitutes Badiou's hypertranslation, which simultaneously sustains and challenges its identity with respect to a start text. This instantiates in a series of mappings from the Greek classic into modern French, which Emily Apter (2013: 22) applauds as demonstrative of 'strong translation'. Badiou's mappings include the transposition of 'Republic' (*République*) into 'State' (*État*) or 'politics' (*politique*); 'God' (*Dieu*) into 'Big Other' (*grand Autre*) or 'Other' (*Autre*); 'soul' (*âme*) into 'Subject' (*Sujet*); and 'Idea of the Good' (*Idée du Bien*) into 'Truth' (*Vérité*). On the basis of these radical shifts across languages, philosophical idioms, and spatial-temporal registers, Apter (2013: 20) hails Badiou's translation as a 'true adventure in philosophy' through which the philosopher 'theatricalizes the mise-en-scène of Platonic discourse ... introduces French slang and ... takes liberties with Plato's content to the point of inventing a new female character'.

On the aesthetic side of things, hypertranslation is closely associated with the longstanding idea of transcreation, borne out of the Brazilian avant-garde movement in the mid twentieth century. Haroldo de Campos's idea of translation as *transcriação* or transcreation first appeared in his 1962 essay 'A tradução como criação e como crítica' [Translation as creation and criticism]. The term was formally introduced in his article 'Tradução, Ideologia e História' (de Campos 1983). Transcreation proposes that translation results in two texts in two languages that maintain an isomorphic relationship (de Campos 1992). On this view, the translator is a writer-creator and the translation is a new, autonomous text. But there is more intensity to the theory than it sounds: translation is *cannibalization*. The latter term is a powerful one, not least because of the violent imagery it evokes; it is understood not as mutilation, but as a symbolic act of love, an act that absorbs the virtues of a foreign body through the transfusion of blood. Cannibalization is an empowering act that destabilizes the original by challenging and inverting the traditional binary opposition between primary and secondary, the author and the translator, and the source and the target (Borowski 2024: 23), thus devouring received conceptions of authority. It is 'an operation of alteration, of becoming ... always becoming, never resolving into being, never wistfully looking back to any stable point of origin' (Gómez 2023: 7). Cannibal translation thus empowers the translator to subvert established power structures (Gómez 2023: 9). It should be noted, though, that translation as cannibalization 'does not conjure away the "original", but devours it in order to create a cultural attitude nourished by foreign influences and enriched by autochthonous input which helps to dismantle the traditional asymmetrical power relations between the cultures involved' (Wolf 2003: 126–27). Cannibal translation develops productive suspicion in the traditional process of translation, and sees this becoming as 'mediated, unfinished, and lovingly disruptive. Cannibal translations refuse readers the comfort of a finished "target text" – and they also call into question any fixed notion of textual originals' (Gómez 2023: 18). In this vein, to transcreate is 'not to try to reproduce the original's form ... but to appropriate the translator's contemporary's best poetry, to use the local existing tradition' (Haroldo de Campos in Vieira 1994: 70).

How does hypertranslation enter this picture? In the essay 'Mephistofaustian Transluciferation (Contributions to the semiotics of poetic translation)', Haroldo de Campos (1982) specifically mentions hypertranslation where he admonishes the translator of poetry 'to hear the beating of the "wild heart" of the art of translation, regarded as a "form": poetic translation, "transcreation", hypertranslation' (p. 184). For de Campos, therefore, hypertranslation is synonymous with transcreation. In discussing his brother Augusto de Campos's translation of *l(a)(a leaf falls on loneliness)* by e.e. cummings, Haroldo de Campos sets out the theoretical parameters of transcreation:

> We may say, then, that every translation of a creative text will always be a 're-creation', a parallel and autonomous, although reciprocal, translation – 'transcreation'. The more intricate the text is, the more seducing it is to 'recreate' it. Of course in a translation of this type, not only the signified but also the sign itself is translated, that is, the sign's tangible self, its very materiality (sonorous properties, graphical-visual properties, all of that which forms, for Charles Morris, the *iconicity* of the aesthetic sign, when an iconic sign is

understood as that which is 'in some degree similar to its denotation'). (de Campos in Bessa & Cisneros 2007: 315; emphasis added)

Here de Campos offers an original imagery of the start text as an open texture attracting translational intervention: the text *seduces*; translation *traduces*. The sexual overtones in this formulation are reified by the emphasis on the materiality of signification, comprising the multisensory resources that make up 'the iconicity of the aesthetic sign', its 'tangible self'. In understanding meaning merely as a field delineating the contours of creative effort, de Campos pivots away from reproducing the semantic substance of signs toward their reconstitution in creative forms – an approach that directly informs our take on hypertranslation. Such is the 'philosophy of translation' espoused by transcreation, one that attends to 'the phono-semantic qualities of the text; to the craftsmanship of the artist-creators, who left signs of their personal creativity in each translation, as if it were the signature of an artist on the canvas; and to translation that crosses literatures and languages' (Jackson 2020: 97).

In their experiments with translation, the de Campos brothers traduce by rewriting a text that is seductive by way of its complexity – '[t]he more intricate the text is, the more seducing it is to "recreate" it' (de Campos in Bessa & Cisneros 2007: 315). The text, then, is a total sign to be transformed by manipulating visual resources on the page, or what we might call optical data such as interlinear relations and typographical spacing. A few examples would suffice to illustrate this. In his 1979 translation of *Faust,* Haroldo de Campos retitled Goethe's work as *Deus e o Diabo no Fausto de Goethe* (God and the Devil in Goethe's *Faust*). According to Vieira, 'the intertext in the very title [in translation] suggests that the receiving culture will interweave and transform the original one' (Vieira 1999: 106). The translator's persona is made eminently visible via paratextual cues; for example, the enumeration of de Campo's, not Goethe's, works at the end of the book under the heading 'Works by the Author' (Vieira 1999: 106). All of this foregrounds the translator's stake in the new language version of Goethe's work. Finally, Augusto de Campos' transcreation of Blake's 'The Sick Rose' (1794), 'A rosa doente' (1978), transforms Blake's poem into a concrete poem by means of an organic translation imbued with great dynamicity: the Portuguese words are shaped dynamically, in constant movement, to form the petals of a flower, into the heart of which the text eventually disappears. The paper, as it were, is a canvas on which Blake's poem is visualized. These radical instances of translation are limit texts; in the words of Augusto de Campos, they are paradoxically 'untranslations' or *intraduçaos* (intraductions, a blending of *introdução* with *tradução*), *prosa porosa* (porous prose) into which sensory information not present in the original can be introduced: *intraduçaos* 'transform the original poem into a sort of physical object, and reveal elements not present in the original text ... Thus the "intraductions" of Augusto de Campos are visual poems, which finally become "translation art"' (Hernández 2010: 153; our translation). His 'untranslations' are political (Brune 2020: 188–89) and 'paradoxically highlight the untranslatable while translating. They introduce but refuse to fully translate longer texts, instead hyperfragmenting the work and inviting readers to investigate what is missing' (Gómez 2023: 20). Hypertranslation, on this view, governs the creation of *intraduçaos* – (un)translations that are non-definitive, non-hierarchical, and non-dualistic. Cannibal transcreations are generative, always becoming intraductions that hold works open, operating on readers 'to require their participation, calling for an attentive, active, suspicious, or contrary reader ... [refusing] to settle into one final version' (Gómez 2023: 217).

Finally, hypertranslation also evokes virtual modalities of communication, taking us on a different pathway toward media studies. The evolution of electronic transmission infrastructures leads to the rise of teletranslation, 'the wholesale shift of T&I [translation and interpreting] to a service based on electronic networks, allowing translators and interpreters to be accessible in cyberspace' (O'Hagan 2001: 100). Extending this development, hyperTranslation (spelled with a capital T by O'Hagan) denotes 'a sophisticated form of distributed language support' comprising 'three-dimensional, albeit virtual, presence-based communication' (p. 100). In such communications, extralinguistic cues are especially critical to signification, which should call to mind real-time interpreting events on Zoom where factors such as eye alignment, tonal variation, gesticulation, and body orientation contribute to meaning-making. It is easy to see how ongoing developments in communication technologies have extended the parameters of electronic translation way beyond the ambit of O'Hagan's teletranslation – developments that we seek to encompass with hypertranslation.

Thus, as it stands, hypertranslation encompasses an array of things, namely:

(a) over-reading in the hermeneutic sense (à la Cook, but positively valued here);
(b) creative adaptation by way of conceptual mapping (à la Badiou);
(c) an emphatic interest in the materiality of signs (à la de Campos); and
(d) the virtualization of interlingual solutions in networked environments (à la O'Hagan).

Consolidating and extending these strands, this Element proposes hypertranslation as a theoretical lens on the heterogeneous, mediational, extrapolative, and networked nature of cultural and knowledge production, especially in cyberspace, arguing that it is a fundamental condition of contemporary communication in Web 5.0 and beyond. Drawing on a wide range of literary and artistic experiments, including those by Jim Rosenberg, Tom Phillips, John Cayley, Eric Zboya, Xu Bing, and Antoni Muntadas, we expound on hypertranslation through the concepts of meme, transmodality, and experientiality, with an eye on the transformational role of digital technology in interlingual, multimodal, and transmedial writing and art. We also consider how developments in artificial intelligence have led to an expansion in intersemiotic potentialities and the liquidation of institutionalized borders. These developments lead to an altered semiotic ecology in which the production, circulation, consumption, and requisition of virtual resources are reaching exponential proportions, wherein the posthumanist condition will be indelibly marked by new translational imaginaries.

2 What Is So *Hyper* about Hypertranslation?

Our conception of hypertranslation is inspired by antecedent terms that share the prefix *hyper-*: most prominently hypertext, but also hyperculture and hyperobject.

2.1 The Hypertext

In Genette's (1997) *Palimpsests*, hypertextuality is one of the five types of transtextual relations, and translation is designated as an exemplar of the hypertext. Although Genette's author-centric understanding of translation would be conservative from today's vantage point, his notion of translation as a hypertext reveals its commentary function, pointing to a connectedness between translation and the capacity to see beyond the text itself. A hypertranslation – which we might gloss as *a hypertext-based understanding of translation* – accords the translator an agentive and critical role (Batchelor 2022: 52). Translations, then, 'are a response to a demand that is not fixed; a commentary that is open, not closed; a living thing' (Batchelor 2022: 59).

Our understanding of hypertext comes more directly from George Landow (1992, 2006), whose idea of the hypertext is traceable to Roland Barthes' *S/Z*. The following passage from *S/Z* encapsulates the workings of the hypertext, and, by our extension, hypertranslation:

> [T]he networks [*réseaux*] are many and interact, without any one of them being able to surpass the rest; this text is a galaxy of signifiers, not a structure of signifieds; it has no beginning; it is reversible; we gain access to it by several entrances, none of which can be authoritatively declared to be the main one; the codes it mobilizes extend *as far as the eye can reach*, they are

indeterminable ... the systems of meaning can take over this absolutely plural text, but their number is never closed, based as it is on the infinity of language. (Barthes 1970/1974: 5–6)

Thus, a hypertext is one 'composed of blocks of text [Barthes's *lexia*] and the electronic links that join them' (Landow 2006: 3); these links create 'multiple paths, chains, or trails in an open-ended, perpetually unfinished textuality described by the terms *link, node, network, web*, and *path*' (Landow 1992: 3), providing 'an infinitely re-centerable system whose provisional point of focus depends upon the reader, who becomes a truly active reader in yet another sense' (Landow 1992: 11). The prototypical hypertext is an electronic research article in which other relevant studies are cited and where each citation established a connection with a different text or set of texts outside the frame of the article. This mode of textuality is marked by spatial non-fixity[2]:

> Unlike the spatial fixity of text reproduced by means of book technology, electronic text always has variation, for no one state or version is ever final; it can always be changed. Compared to a printed text, one in electronic form appears relatively dynamic, since it always permits correction, updating, and similar modification. Even without linking, therefore, electronic text abandons the fixity that characterizes print and that provides some of its most important effects on Western culture. Without fixity one cannot have a unitary text. (Landow 1992: 52)

The hypertext gives rise to multiple routes of reading that emanate from a start text and branch out in different directions; the actual pathway traversed by the reader depends on their particular navigation of the reading space. In this regard the reader is more aptly called a 'user'. Hypertexts thus release reader-users from fixated structures on the page or screen and enable them to organize their own reading trajectory and experience between texts (Landow 1992: 13). More than that: the affordances of digital writing platforms enable reading to become *writerly* in that users can annotate a text they are reading, create spin-offs (as demonstrated by fanzines), and supplement new links or material to the text (Landow 2006: 8–9). Reading in this writerly sense is *rhizomatic* (Landow 2006: 60–62) – branching sideways, making unexpected lateral connections from one node to another (Deleuze & Guattari 1987) – as well as *ergodic* – the user undertakes the 'nontrivial act' of choosing specific pathways of traversal

---

[2] The idea of spatial non-fixity with respect to electronic texts has been criticized by O'Sullivan as illusory: 'Claiming that the "electronic text always has variation" is an example of the illusion in play – all language can have variance. Electronic forms can give the *appearance* of freedom, but *no medium can transcend fixity*. What we tend to see in this field is an element of indeterminacy which changes what is essentially multilinear fiction into something which looks quite different. The difference is the layering, the space, the presence of something which looks to be more than what it actually is' (2019: 81).

within a sprawling network of routes (Aarseth 1997). An ergodic text empowers a reader to alter the outcome of reading through an engaged manipulation of the text – beyond a simple turning of pages. Reading, then, is a traversal of the materiality of the text, which can be reimagined rather as a game to be played by making selections that draw out different resources – think, for instance, how one traverses the virtual space in Pokémon GO through physical action (Guo et al. 2022). An ergodic reading is multimodal, encompassing words, images, maps, diagrams, sounds, and perhaps (if we dare imagine) even movements and smells. In this sense, hypertext is coextensive with Landow's (2006: 3) 'hypermedia'.

Coover (1992) gives us important clues as to the operation of hypertexts. Following Barthes, he argues that the hypertext provides multiple paths between text segments. It is interactive and polyvocal and it favours that readers and writers become co-learners and co-writers. He is committed to the 'subversion of the traditional bourgeois novel and in fictions that challenge linearity' and prefers a kind of literature that is infinitely expandable, infinitely alluring webs with gardens of multiple forking paths – the latter image alludes to Jorge Luis Borges, who is 'popular with hypertext buffs'. Coover highlights how much of the reading and writing experience 'occurs in the interstices and trajectories between text fragments. That is to say, the text fragments are like stepping stones, there for our safety, but the real current of the narratives runs between them' (n. p.). An example is Coover's 'The Babysitter', a story in fragments with a non-traditional multilinear narrative structure. It contains shifts in point of view, multiple narrative paths that rewrite the events within the story. This was a model for later hypertexts (see Rettberg 2019 for this and many other examples of combinatory poetics, hypertext fiction, and interactive literature).

2.1.1 Jim Rosenberg's Non-linear Poetry

The hypertext is exemplified by Jim Rosenberg's non-linear poetic forms in different media. Rosenberg is a well-known experimental artist, influenced by John Cage and the Concrete Poets, who works with different compositional styles. *Intergrams* (1988–1992), made of 'interactive word space, overlaid layers as simultaneities, locus identical, word clusters at last, linked through a diagram-work syntax with all slots open, verb where the pointing goes, depth on depth, inwardly reaching tokens to the mesh'.[3] His web page contains links to some of his collected interactive work, from the period roughly 1988–2013 (see also Rosenberg 2015). In these works, interactivity is used to introduce

---

[3] www.inframergence.org/jr/Intergrams_desc.shtml.

multiplicities into word space. Many of these works are made available as multiplatform downloads, for a wide variety of computer operating systems. These works may be considered hypertexts – in the broad sense of the word, 'though they are certainly not simply "nodes and links" – the primitive concept many people think is all there is to hypertext'.[4] His lifelong series of diagram poems are relevant here. For instance, Rosenberg explains how juxtaposition, interactivity, and multiplicity are essential in his *Diagrams Series 6*. They are written in one interactive environment 'where the word object is playable at every stage of its development, from temporary unassembled scrap all the way to its final location in a finished piece. This environment is part of an ongoing project which I call Hypertext in the Open Air, and is implemented in a programming system called Squeak'.[5]

Rosenberg's poem *The Inframergence* (2007–2013), inspired by the contemplation of two Monets in the Denver Art Museum, is another illustration of hypertextual non-linearity. The outer interface of *The Inframergence* is a spiral of buttons arranged chronologically in the order written, from the outside in. Each button leads to polylinear screens, to skeins that stretch across the space:

> But stretch *within* a space; as the cursor moves off of the skein, the skein recedes to the back, its pair-mate comes to the front, reading in the opposite direction: boustrophedon of resonance, linear by internal sequence but travel inverted, the eye thus moving but at place. Travel but non-travel. Linear for resonance fall but not navigation.
>
> As you move to the inside of the spiral, the screens become less and less linear. The skein parts coalesce. Then become word clusters, of a kind I have used many times. Then structure begins to emerge: a structure of simple dominance/receding, mediation through. This structure is a form of proto-syntax; in a way *The Inframergence* is a kind of 'prequel' to the diagram notation used in much of my work. At the screens that launch from the innermost buttons of the spiral, larger spaces collapse to icons, which are buttons which expand to the 'open' state; this collapsing and opening preserves spatial relationships, making a kind of 'spatial stretchtext'.
>
> The spiral is thus a kind of evolution-in, structure and structure evasion together, in close confines, interoperating. The oscillation. Not a contradiction, but scaffold and chorus-brushed flock, granular, together but separate, intact but chorded.
>
> Infrawhere.[6]

Thus, the poet's layered language, his integration of the visual with the semantic, results in a particular kind of language, in collage, in interactive works

---

[4] www.inframergence.org/jr/inter_works.shtml.   [5] www.inframergence.org/jr/d6_desc.shtml.
[6] www.inframergence.org/jr/Inframergence_desc.shtml.

where a word is placed upon another to show simultaneity, multiplicity, and erasure, since these words disappear as time passes. His clusters of words remind one of John Cage's tone clusters. His aim is to achieve a 'spatial stretchtext' that is open, multiple, and always in motion. It is the qualities of interactivity, multiplicity, openness, oscillation, and contradiction immanent to Rosenberg's works that make them hypertextual.

2.1.2 Tom Phillips's A Humument

Tom Phillips's *A Humument* is a particularly interesting example of non-sequentiality and multilinearity. To create it, Phillips employed the same technique as authors such as Nick Thurston whose novel, *Reading the Remove of Literature* (2006), was written from the English translation of Maurice Blanchot's *L'Espace littéraire* (1955).[7]

Phillips places his 'Author's Preface' at the end instead of the beginning of the novel. In those opening/final pages of the last edition of the novel, 'Notes on A Humument' (Phillips 2016: n. p.), the author states that it is a book created out of chance and serendipity. In 1966 Phillips bet with his friend, R.B. Kitaj that he would use the first book that he came across that cost less than three pence as the basis of 'a serious long-term project' (Phillips 2016: n. p.). The book finally chosen for this purpose was *A Human Document*, by W. H. Mallock (1892), a grey and rather boring Victorian novel that Phillips had never heard of. Influenced by William Burrough's and John Cage's use of chance, Phillips chose not to read the novel as an ordered story. As he observes, 'Though in some sense I almost know the whole of it by heart, I have to this day never read it properly from beginning to end' (Phillips 2016: n. p.). The title, like so much else in the novel, arose from pure chance:

> The book's rechristening resulted from another chance discovery. By folding one page in half and turning it back to reveal half of the following page, the running title at the top abridged itself to A HUMUMENT, an earth word with echoes of humanity and monument as well as a sense of something hewn, or exhumed to end up in the muniment rooms of the archived world. (Phillips 2016: n. p.)

---

[7] Other examples of hypertext include Kristen Muller's *Partially Removing the Remove of Literature* (2014), a palimpsest created from Thurston's palimpsest, and Derek Beaulieu's *a, A Novel* (2017), a digitally erasured translative response to Warhol's *a, A Novel* (1968). Also worth mentioning are Ronald Johnson's *Radi os* (1977), a rewriting by excision of the first four books of the 1892 edition of John Milton's *Paradise Lost,* and Jen Bervin's *The Desert* (2008), an art piece in which Bervin sews with blue thread over the 'erased' words of John Van Dyke's *The Desert* (1901). It is also a palimpsest because the 'original' is still visible beneath the threads. Nor should we forget Jen Bervin's *Nets* (2003), Jonathan Safran Foer's *Tree of Codes* (2010), and Austin Kleon's *Newspaper Blackout* (2010), among others.

Although initially, Phillips had no intention of including any outside elements in Mallock's novel, little by little he found himself incorporating outside material, motifs, and collaged imagery. *A Humument* thus became an entirely new work in which every page of the previous novel has been altered through painting, collage, and cut-and-paste techniques. Phillips isolates words and phrases 'to (de)construct his text, while painting over & illuminating the remainder of each page (sometimes in many versions) with images ranging in one instance "from a telegram envelope to a double copy of a late Cézanne landscape"' (Rothenberg & Joris 1998: 630).

The process of constructing his text from the previous one evolved over the years. This is hardly surprising since the novel was started in 1966 and its final version was not published until 2016. The name of the hero was also randomly assigned, and his story is equally non-linear. Nor does his appearance in the novel respond to 'logical' reasons of plot development, but rather to others more related to chance:

> A hidden hero emerged from behind the text to interact with the novel's actual protagonists. Since W in W. H. Mallock stands for William, its commonplace short form, Bill, provided a good matey name for his humdrum alter ego. When I chanced on 'bill' it appeared next to the word 'altogether' and thus the downmarket and blokeish name Bill Toge was born. It became a rule that Toge should appear wherever the words 'together' or 'altogether' occurred. (Phillips 2016: n. p.)

In 1969, the novel provided the draft score of an opera. Then in 1973, the first version was published, in which Phillips had already altered every page. This first version of all 367 'treated pages' was displayed at the Institute of Contemporary Arts in London and subsequently in other exhibitions. It was even displayed at the Royal Academy, where each page was framed as though it were a work of art. It goes without saying that this way of showcasing the book also raised the unspoken question of whether it is indeed a piece of visual art. In 2010, it went on to enter the digital world with *The Humument App*, launched by Phillips for the iPad (followed by *A Humument App* for the iPhone in 2011). The App combines 367 full-colour pages with an interactive feature called 'The Oracle', which selects random pages to generate daily messages about the reader's 'fate and fortune':

> Using a date and a randomly generated number the oracle will cast two pages to be read in tandem. Like the I Ching, the ancient Chinese *Book of Changes*, chance pairs of pages, taken together and interpreted, act as a guide and cryptic commentary on life in word and picture. 'The Oracle', more playful than serious, offers direction. There is amusement in the game but watch out for the odd uncanny prophecy. You can email your personal choices or oracle

reading to friends, or post them to your Facebook, Tumblr or Twitter profile direct from the App.[8]

Phillips's *A Humument* is a hypertranslation because it is a constantly multiplied, multilayered, and multidimensional work on the basis of a start text. A palimpsest which has been the take-off point for the creation of many other works in different media, for example, the already mentioned opera *Irma,*

> with libretto, music, staging instructions, & costume design all coming from *A Human Document*; a fully illustrated edition of Dante's Inferno (in Phillips's verse translation); a video version of the Inferno's first eight cantos (called A TV Dante), with Peter Greenaway as codirector; numerous musical works like the Six of Hearts sequence, written for soprano Mary Wiegold and the Composers' Ensemble (London), the singer selecting its six texts from the previously published *A Heart of a Humument*; & above all, over a thousand visual/verbal texts extracted from the source work. (Rothenberg & Joris 1998: 630)

With the continuous transformations that the novel has undergone, Phillips has incorporated new meanings in keeping with the times. For example, from the penultimate page of *A Human Document* Phillips extracts Joyce's famously repeated 'Yes' at the end of *Ulysses*; in 2011, he found in Mallock's novel both 'app' and 'facebook', and Phillips included those words on page 9 of his hypertranslation in the phrases 'three miniatures in her facebook' and 'in the app of this volume', which would have been impossible in the 1960s. Phillips also mentions that at the beginning of his endeavour he could not have predicted 'the dark resonance the "bush" suddenly came to have or how a simple word like "net" would grow immeasurably in significance' (Phillips 2016: n. p.). As pointed out by the author, the last two versions of the novel could not have existed before the events that they reflect because language is constantly changing. This is evident in his tribute to the #MeToo movement in which four red-and-green hashtags frame a watercolour portrait of a woman. Although the visual language is a constant in all the versions of the novel, quite strikingly, in the sixth edition nearly every page has been changed. Page 4 is particularly relevant here because it illustrates in a very complex and multilayered fashion Phillips's urge to react to the attacks on the Twin Towers in New York in 2001. The way he creates that page is a clear example of what we are calling hypertranslation. As Phillips recalls:

> Many years ago I had a concordance made ... of the whole novel in a little notebook now frayed and stained to the point of unusability. This was replaced by an electronically created version masterminded by John Pull

---

[8] www.printmag.com/daily-heller/introducing-the-humuapp/.

and smartly bound, which I duly searched for the unlikely occurrence of 'nine' and 'eleven' on the same page in the right order. To my amazement I found them, on the yet to be reworked p4. As has always been my practice, I look for a text first and let its disposition condition any imagery that is at the back of my mind. In this case, I scanned the page on the lookout for opposite commentary. I recalled the event's uncanny prefigurement in the *Inferno* where Dante compares the giant Anteus to the skyscrapers of his day, the bristling skyline of 13th-century Florence with its many tall and narrow towers. A postcard of King Kong was already featured clutching at the World Trade Center in *A Postcard Century*, as was a version of Goya's *Saturn Devouring his Children*. These pictures were thus 'pasted on to the present' as the text suggests. The accompanying Roman numerals make a twinning palindrome and their non-arabic presence suggests the 'time singular' also mentioned.

Thus classical mythology joins medieval poetry together with an early 19th-century Spanish painting, a Victorian novel and a 20th-century American film, linking late modern architecture to a 21st-century disaster. (Phillips 2016: n. p.)

Phillips's hypertranslation tells a dispersed story with more than one possible order, 'more like a pack of cards than a continuous tale. Even in the revision I still have not tackled the pages in numerical order' (Phillips 2016: n. p.). Furthermore, the process of transformation has continued over the years, 'with *Humument* fragments providing gores for fictitious globes (now in the Victoria & Albert Museum) or decorating both the inside and outside of a skull. Most recently, excerpts have accompanied an illustrated edition of Cicero's *Orations* made for the Folio Society' (Phillips 2016: n. p.). It could effectively be said that Phillips's stand-alone collages, paintings, decorated skulls, and other of his creations, are hypertranslations of *A Humument*. Over the years, *A Human Document* has pervaded Phillips's creations beyond the scope of *A Humument*. 'In the end the work became an attempt to make a *Gesamtkunstwerk* in small format, since it includes poems, music scores, parodies, notes on aesthetics, autobiography, concrete texts, romance, mild erotica, as well as the undertext of Mallock's original story'. (Phillips in Rothenberg & Joris 1998: 630).

In her analysis of *A Humument*, Katherine Hayles points out that Phillips implements strategies similar to Mallock's. In the introduction of *A Human Document*, Mallock creates a narrator who explains that the novel tells the story of two dead lovers, Irma and Grenville, based on scrapbooks of journals, letters, and other documents they had left behind and which he had come across one day. Thus, according to Hayles (2002: 78), Phillips 'seeks to bring into view again this suppressed hypertextual profusion' (Hayles 2002: 78). By not coining new words but obliterating ones that already exist, Phillips's intention seems to be 'to silence the rationalizing consciousness of narrator and editor so that the murmurs of hypertextual resistance to coherent narrative can be heard' (Hayles 2002: 81). Hayles views the 'rivers' of text as a reference to both hypertextual paths of reading and the possibilities of multiple treatment of a single page:

> Visually these rivers of white space trickle down the page, often branching into multiple pathways. Other devices creating hypertextual profusion are leaky borders, which visually separate the page into multiple narrative levels and also transgress this separation, suggesting that distinctions between character, narrator and author are less ontological categories than contingent boundaries susceptible to multiple reconfiguration. Additional hypertextual effects are achieved through interplays between word and image. (Hayles 2002: 81)

In the terms developed in this Element, *A Humument* is a hypertext because of its narrative multiplicity, constant displacements, and infinite possible reading sequences: 'Broken and reassembled, the prose achieves the compression of poetry, becoming allusive and metaphoric rather than sequentially coherent' (Hayles 2002: 82). Since the book is endless, it has infinite possible readings. It is a palimpsest that never ends, as the author himself states in his note (Phillips 2016: n. p.): 'In order to prove (to myself) the inexhaustibility of even a single page I started a set of variations on page 85: I have already made over twenty'. In his constant revision of *A Humument,* he creates new pages that he puts up at his website before the printed editions appear. For Phillips, Mallock's text is an infinite hypertext (Hayles 2002: 88).

According to Hayles, the fact that Phillips used chance to read Mallock's book, and also that he never read it following the established order, from beginning to end, encourages the reader not to read it that way either, but rather to open it at random. All these features convert *A Humument* into what Hayles calls, using modern terminology, 'the original random access device (RAD). Contrary to much hype about electronic hypertext, books like *A Humument* allow the reader considerably more freedom of movement and access than do many electronic fictions. In this respect, the book is more RAD than most computer texts – a conclusion that the bibliophiles among us will relish' (Hayles 2002: 99).

2.2 Hyperculture and Hyperobject

We have seen that the hypertext represents non-sequentiality and multilinearity. It prioritizes intertextual linkages that enable users to 'find, create, and follow multiple conceptual structures in the same body of information' (Landow 2006: 10). This entails a transgression of boundaries constructed by political and institutional discourses to delineate, categorize, and manage cultural phenomena including languages, modes, and media. Which brings us to the concept of hyperculture, defined by Byung-Chul Han (2022a) as an immanently heterogeneous culture 'organized not by borders but by links and network connections' (p. 9) – in other words, by rhizomes. What ensues is a *sitelessness*, a siteless site that is 'un-bound, unrestricted, unravelled' (p. 9), a symptom of the liquid times in which we live (Bauman 2007). Our twenty-first-century society has moved from a solid hardware to a liquid software (Bauman 2000). Our contemporary world is made up of many worlds which become interrelated and irremissibly linked together. A world that has overcome traditional binarist dialectics and solid and fixed definitions and which prefers fluid borders, and liquid definitions, while it takes pleasure in mixing, joining, and bringing into conflict different ways of looking at the world (Bauman 2007). We inhabit a liquid epistemology in Bauman's (2000: 9) sense of the word, because structures, patterns, and institutions, 'can no longer (and are not expected) to keep their shape for long, because they decompose and melt faster than the time it takes to cast them ... Forms ... are unlikely to be given enough time to solidify, and cannot serve as frames of reference for human actions and long-term life strategies' (Bauman 2007: 1). In this context, Bauman (2007: 3) argues, 'society' is viewed as a 'network' rather than a 'structure' or a 'totality': 'it is perceived and treated as a matrix of random connections and (disconnections) and of an essentially infinite volume of possible permutations'. Liquidity brings about altered chronotopes (i.e., timespaces; see Blommaert 2015) where temporality is marked by the ephemeral, the contingent, and the non-permanent; and spatiality by a de-territorialization (Deleuze & Guattari 1980/1987) under which signs are released from fixated forms and susceptible to transduction (Kress & van Leeuwen 2021: 38).

Hyperculture is the broader epistemological milieu in which hypertranslation arises. We thus conceive of hypertranslation not primarily as an isolated technique in translation but as a fundamental semiotic condition of our times, one that is immanently and radically creative (see Malmkjær 2020: 3). Yet hypertranslation is not a permanent condition, but a temporary, transient, and transformative one, an *inter-esse,* that state of betweenness Deleuze and Guattari understand as the medium, the interference. It is a not purely linear, singular, cohesive, and process, but comprises entangled lines, multiplicities, and complex continuations along other lines: 'we are composed of lines, three kinds of lines. Or rather, of bundles of lines, for each is multiple' (Deleuze & Guattari 1980/1987: 202). Thus, hypertranslating means 'making the world a becoming':

> becoming-everybody/everything, making the world a becoming, is to world, to make a world or worlds, in other words, to find one's proximities and zones of indiscernibility. The Cosmos as an abstract machine, and each world as an assemblage effectuating it. If one reduces oneself to one or several abstract lines that will prolong itself in and conjugate with others, producing immediately, directly *a* world in which it is *the* world that becomes, then one becomes-everybody/everything. (Deleuze & Guattari 1980/1987: 280)

Hypertranslation shows translation as a map, one that 'fosters connections between fields … open and connectable in all of its dimensions; it is detachable, reversible, susceptible to constant modification' (Deleuze & Guattari 1980/1987: 12). Hypertranslation is a *chaosmos*, a term first coined by James Joyce and taken up by Deleuze and Guattari as representing the cyclic dance of creation in constant movement between chaos and cosmos, between order and disorder. Hence chaosmosis, 'the uncanny valley of vagueness and opacity, an equivocation of order and disorder' (Zanelli 2022: 47; see also Genosko 2002: 194–216). One should bear in mind that, according to Deleuze, chaos is the element in which thought 'never ceases to float and which must continually be counteracted'; it is not simply the absence of order, 'but an affirmation that *chaotizes* and that dissolves the knots of consistency associated with regularity' (Zanelli 2022: 50).

Hypertranslation creates assemblages in Deleuze and Guattari's (1980/1987) sense.[9] It is a multiplicity of multiplicities, an always multiple and rhizomatic process that 'emerges from the continual interactions of its heterogeneous component parts' (Seddon 2019: 107). As an assemblage, it

> necessarily changes in nature as it expands its connections. There are no points or positions in a rhizome, such as those found in a structure, tree, or root. There are only lines … The number is no longer a universal concept measuring elements according to their emplacement in a given dimension, but has itself become a multiplicity that varies according to the dimensions considered (the primacy of the domain over a complex of numbers attached to that domain). We do not have units (unites) of measure, only multiplicities or varieties of measurement. The notion of unity (unite) appears only when there

---

[9] Katherine Hayles (2021: 13) also uses the term 'assemblage' drawing on the work of both Bruno Latour and Gilles Deleuze and Félix Guattari, albeit with some differences. Also interesting to note here is Tanasescu's (2024b) ideas on the intersection of digital humanities and translation from the perspectives of anthologies (see also Tanasescu & Tanasescu 2023). This is related to Tanasescu's work on Jerome Rothenberg, as well as her co-translations of Rothenberg's work into Romanian with Chris Tanasescu. Rothenberg's struggle against the canonical anthologies. He uses the form 'as a kind of manifesto-assemblage: to present, to bring to light, or to create works that have been excluded or that collectively present a challenge to the dominant system-makers or to the world at large' (Rothenberg 2006: 16). All the anthologies he has assembled are therefore 'a detournement (a turning or a twist) on the structures & presumptions of those fixed anthologies that continue (like the darkness) to surround us' (Rothenberg 2006: 17).

is a power takeover in the multiplicity by the signifier or a corresponding subjectification proceeding. (Deleuze & Guattari 1980/1987: 8)

In fact, assemblage in the sense of Deleuze and Guattari is the best way to conceptually describe a computational approach to literary texts, since it has to do with constant becoming, with mutation, with the French term *agencement*, used by Deleuze as a dynamic concept related to the process of fitting together an assemblage, not as a set of predetermined parts put together into a preconceived structure but as a becoming (see Tanasescu 2024b: 97).

Like assemblages, hypertranslations are always in constant variation, constantly subject to transformation and decentring the sovereign human subject. Hypertranslations act through Deleuzean 'affect' and thus interact and intermingle with humans, non-humans, earth beings, animate and inanimate things. An example could be the non-human 'writers' in the works of the Chinese artist and book designer Zhu Yingchun, 'author' of *The Language of Bugs* (2018) and *Cacaform Birds* (2019). *The Language of Bugs* is here a particularly relevant example because it is 'written' with no words, using the natural characters and movements of bugs, who translate information in their own way. The book is thus made completely from the perspective and 'language' of bugs, featuring not human writing but the marks and traces left behind by a cicada walking across the sketchbook.[10]

No doubt, this is diametrically different from any binary perspective: it is rhizomatic, without a linear structure, generative, and constantly intermingling with no centre to speak of. It eschews 'reductionist explanations of top-down structural authority' (Seddon 2019: 111), constantly within ongoing territorializing and deterritorializing processes. In *A Thousand Plateaus*, Deleuze and Guattari are fascinated by the relationship between the wasp and certain orchids:

> The orchid deterritorializes by forming an image, a tracing of a wasp; but the wasp reterritorializes on that image. The wasp is nevertheless deterritorialized, becoming a piece in the orchid's reproductive apparatus. But it reterritorializes the orchid by transporting its pollen. Wasp and orchid, as heterogeneous elements, form a rhizome. It could be said that the orchid imitates the wasp, reproducing its image in a signifying fashion (mimesis, mimicry, lure, etc.). But this is true only on the level of the strata – a parallelism between two strata such that a plant organization on one imitates an animal organization on the other. At the same time, something else entirely is going on: not imitation at all but *a capture of code, surplus value of code, an increase in valence, a veritable becoming, a becoming-wasp of the orchid and a becoming-orchid of the wasp*. Each of these becomings brings about the

---

[10] www.zhuyingchun.com/books.

deterritorialization of one term and the reterritorialization of the other; the two becomings interlink and form relays in a circulation of intensities pushing the deterritorialization ever further. There is neither imitation nor resemblance, only an exploding of two heterogeneous series on the line of flight composed by a common rhizome that can no longer be attributed to or subjugated by anything signifying. (Deleuze & Guattari 1980/1987: 10; emphasis added)

Like the wasp's relationship with the orchid, hypertranslation relates unlike entities without uniting them, distinct sensations that participate in 'an infinite symphonic plane of composition' (Deleuze & Guattari 1984: 185). Hypertranslation is thus conceived as a 'becoming-other', producing 'a surplus value of code, an increase in valence'. Hypertranslation can thus be understood as a biological narrative of becoming between the wasp and the orchid. The orchid is becoming-wasp and the wasp is becoming-orchid. In this becoming, movements of deterritorialization and processes of reterritorialization are always connected, since the orchid does not reproduce the tracing of the wasp; it forms a map with the wasp (Deleuze & Guattari 1980/1987: 10). What distinguishes the map from the tracing 'is that it is entirely oriented toward an experimentation in contact with the real' (Deleuze & Guattari 1980/1987: 12).

One can therefore posit a distinction between a singular, formal instantiation of text – what Roland Barthes (1984/1986) calls 'work' – and a floating signifier (*not* signified) that cuts across one or more works, what Barthes calls Text. This floating signifier, in a manner of speaking, is akin to Tim Morton's (2013) hyperobject, which refers to 'things that are massively distributed in time and space relative to humans' (p. 1). Ranging from 'the sum of all the whirring machinery of capitalism' to the universe of planetary bodies, hyperobjects have three common properties. First, viscosity: hyperobjects '"stick" to beings that are involved with them'. Second, nonlocality: hyperobjects, in virtue of their extended temporalities, 'occupy a high-dimensional phase space that results in their being invisible to humans for stretches of time'. Lastly, interobjectivity: hyperobjects to arise within a space that 'consists of interrelationships between aesthetic properties of objects' (Morton 2013: 1).

2.3 Hypertranslation: A Profile

By way of analogy and combining insights from the constructs of hypertext, hyperculture, and hyperobject, we propose hypertranslation as a perspective from which translation can be conceived as:

(a) **nonlocal**: Hypertranslation itself does not denote any specific translation or procedure in translation. Like Barthes's Text, it is a 'methodological field' (Barthes 1984/1986: 58). It is 'not coexistence of meaning, but passage, traversal; hence, it depends not on an interpretation, however liberal, but on an explosion, on dissemination' (p. 59). It subsists as a perpetual liquidity.

(b) **unbounded**: Hypertranslation emerges from the transgression of constructed boundaries traditionally defining 'sites' of inscription (e.g., print, multimedia art, installation, etc.). It is a *siteless site* in which translators creatively and critically experiment with all linguistic and semiotic resources at their disposal across languages, modes, and media. It also transgresses the boundary between human and non-human actants.

(c) **viscous**: Hypertranslation entails, but is not coextensive with, a modality of translation where one text transcends the manifest form – any combination of language, mode, and medium – of another text and so is not directly that latter text; still, the two texts call upon or resonate with each other viscously by way of sharing semiotic traces (called memes: Section 3.1), however tenuous they might be.

(d) **rhizomatic**: Hypertranslation arises when a text (a node) connects translationally with any number of other texts (nodes), which connect to yet other texts ad infinitum to form a networked assemblage, in line with Actor Network Theory (ANT; Latour 2005).

(e) **interobjective**: If a text is perceived as a kind of object, hypertranslation lies in the discursive space between rhizomatically connected textual objects, within the 'interrelationships between aesthetic properties' (Morton 2013: 1).

(f) **ergodic**: The ergodic, as explained earlier, refers to non-trivial interventions that open multiple pathways of textual engagement, in turn influencing reading outcomes. Hypertranslations involve creating rhizomatic connections between texts created by ergodic translators who undertake non-trivial acts of translating – namely, any act of making connections beyond the straight transfer of meaning. Rhizomatic connections form multiple simultaneous pathways of production and consumption contingent upon all the circumstances around a translational event (e.g., adaptation, audio description, localization, fansubbing, and so forth). In virtue of this contingency, hypertranslation takes the analytical focus away from the final translation output, which is but the fleeting outcome of a momentary intervention.

It is worth reiterating that hypertranslation is proposed as a vantage point from which we might appreciate the ontology of translation in contemporary communications. It is not a discrete translation procedure that can be applied or disapplied, but rather a perspective on the translationality between creative moments. Translation, we submit, is in need of further articulation in light of ground-breaking technologies of communication that change our perception of textuality. A theoretical case for this may be made by returning to Barthes's (1984/1986) distinction between a work and a Text. Whereas a work is finite in constitution and 'closes upon a signified' (p. 58), a Text 'cannot stop (for example, at a library shelf); its constitutive moment is traversal (notably, it can traverse the work, several works)' (p. 58). A work is palpable to the senses: it can be read or viewed or listened to. In contrast, a Text is 'experienced only in an activity, in a production' and 'in relation to the sign' (p. 58). Consequently, a Text cannot actually be pinned down, because

> the engendering of the perpetual signifier ... in the *field* of the Text is not achieved by some organic process of maturation, or a hermeneutic process of 'delving deeper', but rather by *a serial movement of dislocations, overlappings, variations*; the logic governing the Text is not comprehensive (trying to define what the work 'means') but *metonymic*; the activity of *associations, contiguities, crossreferences* coincides with a liberation of symbolic energy. (Barthes 1984/1986: 59; emphasis added)

In *Roland Barthes by Roland Barthes* Barthes expands the opposition *readerly/ writerly* he used in *S/Z:* 'A *readerly* text is one I cannot rewrite (can I write today like Balzac?); a *writerly* text is one I read with difficulty, unless I completely transform my reading regime', says Barthes (1975/1977: 118). Then he conceives that there may be a third textual entity:

> [A]longside the readerly and the writerly, there would be something like the *receivable*. The *receivable* would be the unreaderly text which catches hold, the red-hot text, a product continuously outside of any likelihood and whose function – visibly assumed by its *scriptor* – would be to contest the mercantile constraint of what is written; this text, guided, armed by a notion of the *unpublishable,* would require the following response: I can neither read nor write what you produce, but I *receive* it, like a fire, a drug, an enigmatic disorganization. (Barthes 1975/1977: 118)

Hypertranslation is 'receivable' insomuch as it contests the constraints of what is written: it seeks to be received as an unpredictable entropy, 'an enigmatic disorganization'. Substituting translation for work and hypertranslation for Text, might we not postulate an analogical relation between translation as a materialized form, 'a fragment of substance' (Barthes 1984/1986: 57), and translation as a continuous flux, a 'methodological field' (p. 58)? Thus defined, hypertranslation points to a contingent and dynamic interplay of signs in which *translation as method* forms the nexus of rhizomatic networks and ephemeral, 'receivable' outcomes. The potential of this conception will come into higher relief when we examine translation against developments in AI and hyperreality technologies in a later section.

3 Hypertranslational Re-readings of Language Art

Hypertranslation is not some new object of study. It is rather a new lens through which existing and prospective creative practices can be transgressively reimagined with an angle on the multiplex connections and emergent transformations driven by material and technological affordances. Before we proceed with the theory, let us revisit the works of two well-known artists, Xu Bing and Antoni Muntadas, to demonstrate how hypertranslation may help us flesh out the conceptual economy of experimental language art.

3.1 Xu Bing

Xu Bing's *Book from the Sky* (1987–1991) is a floor-to-ceiling compilation of traditionally bound manuscripts, of words-images which surround the visitor. We literally plunge into language, or at least into shapes and forms we look at and intuitively identify as language.[11] At first sight the visitor feels language but then realizes that this language fails to communicate, since Xu Bing's pictograph characters are invented, made-up signifiers, untranslatable beautiful scrolls of fabricated texts. At the same time, each character was carefully designed by Xu Bing in a Song-style font that was standardized by artisans in the Ming dynasty. There is a tension because of the illusion of being real language, between what at first sight are familiar signifiers and the disruption of all our literacy expectations (Liu 2011: 122). And we sense, see and nearly touch this disruption, this 'unreadable' book (Cayley 2009, 2015). Xu Bing urges the visitor to realize how often we are surrounded by language as an institutional imposition. Language can also be devoid of content. Words, words, words. But it is also a weapon cornering us, literally surrounding our bodies. Xu spent nearly four years hand carving four thousand nonsensical characters in

---

[11] John Cayley (2009: 1–2) describes *Book from the Sky* as 'not an object' nor 'a painting or a sculpture or even a book as such': 'It's a configuration of objects and materials that represent a concept ... You can't possess it. You either have to find some elaborate way to acquire a personal record of the work or you have to take part in a process that allows the installation to remove itself into a museum or major gallery where this representation, beyond an individual's acquisitive capacities, can be preserved for collective curated culture'. See also Cayley (2015).

this four-volume treatise made of reconfigured Chinese radicals that provoke a critical reconsideration of dominant epistemologies.

In this regard, it is also relevant to mention Xu Bing's *A Case Study of Transference* (1993–1994), a performance and video with two live pigs inked with invented English and Chinese characters on the female and invented English words on the male. It has to do with access to knowledge, with how knowledge is imposed upon us.[12] The pigs are thus transformed into

> vehicles of culture by the imprinting of letters and characters onto their bodies, their sexual union became a symbol of cultural transference. The western Anglophone and the Chinese culture unify in the image of copulating pigs. The male West passes his cultural heritage on to the receptive, female China. The union of the text bodies suggests Chinglish as a transcultural language of understanding. Or, should we see the performed sexual act as a rape, a domination of Chinese culture by the western Anglophone culture? On closer inspection, the union between the cultures turns out to be a farce and a fiction. (Mersmann 2019: 56)

Expanding on the model of the square word calligraphy, *Living Word* (2001–2022) translates that model from the two-dimensionality of the written page or scroll into the three-dimensionality of life-like animated script. It comprises over 400 calligraphic variants of the Chinese character *niao*, meaning bird,

> carved in colored acrylic and laid out in a shimmering track that rises from the floor into the air. On the gallery floor Chinese characters in the 'simplified style' script popularized during the Mao era are used to write out the dictionary definition for *niao*. The bird/*niao* characters then break away from the confines of the literal definition and take flight through the installation space. As they rise into the air, the characters 'de-evolve' from the simplified system to standardized Chinese text and finally to the ancient Chinese pictograph [based] upon a bird's actual appearance. At the uppermost point of the installation, a flock of these ancient characters, in form of both bird and word, soar high into the rafters toward the upper windows of the space, as though attempting to break free of the words with which humans attempt to categorize and define them.
>
> The colorful, shimmering imagery of the installation imparts a magical, fairy-tale like quality. Yet the overt simplicity, charm and ready comprehensibility of the work has the underlying effect of guiding the audience to open up the 'cognitive space' of their minds to the implications of, and relationships between, word, concept, symbol and image.[13]

---

[12] *Cultural Animal* (1994) was created as an extension of *A Case Study of Transference*. It is a performance media installation with a live pig and a live-sized mannequin, both covered in false-character tattoos.

[13] https://www.xubing.com/.

Xu Bing's living words do not provide logical answers. Rather, they are unbounded and rhizomatic. Definitions are not constrained but take an ergodic flight through the installation space. The idea is to create an open, rhizomatic space characterized by the unmediated experience of knowledge and by catalysing non-dual states of mind. This makes clear that for Xu, translation understood as linguistic equivalence is not possible as he highlights the importance of creativity within translation.

Book from the Ground (2013) is a short story without words but with an abundance of pictograms. It is composed entirely of symbols and icons that are, supposedly, universally understood. The book is a meticulous account of twenty-four hours in the life of a typical urban white-collar worker. We 'hear' (see? watch?) how a nearby bird and his alarm clock wakes him up, how he brushes his teeth, how he has breakfast, takes the subway, works in his office, sends e-mails, uses Facebook, Twitter, Google, eats fast-food, watches TV, and feeds his cat. But we also 'see' his emotions, and his daydreams: he sends flowers, socializes, visits a friend who is ill, looks for a partner on the internet, kills a mosquito, and dreams of video game characters at night. The idea is that the quotidian daily activities of this contemporary Leopold Bloom can be understood (universally?) by everybody with no need of translation. Are these icons universal, are these pictograms really understood in the same way by everybody?

Whereas *Book from the Sky* cannot be understood by anyone, *Book from the Ground* can be approached by anyone. However, is it possible to understand these more than 8,000 icons universally? Xu Bing Studio created a character database software that is essentially an intersemiotic machine translator: 'Users can enter words either in English or in Chinese, and subsequently, the program will translate them into Xu Bing's lexicon of signs. It thus serves as an intermediary form of communication and exchange between the two languages. As persona computers and the internet become increasingly integrated into daily life, the lexicon of digital icons grows accordingly, and the symbolic language of *Book from the Ground* has been further updated, augmented, and complexified'.[14] *Book from the Ground* exemplifies the ethos of hypertranslation because

> it takes the form of an interactive exhibit that models on Internet chatting. The inspiration for the project came initially from airline safety manuals and chewing gum wrappers, in which icons take the place of verbal language in what the artist sees as a minimalist and therefore ideal mode of communication. (Lee 2015: 114)

---

[14] https://www.xubing.com/.

Xu Bing's icon-logos, symbols, and pictograms, as designed for *Book from the Ground*, are a new system of communication and translation, although one may doubt the possibility of a global, universal language, and consequently a universal translation out of Xu's icon-script. Nevertheless, the vision is for a translation system enabling 'language-image translation and human digital communication beyond linguistic translation. With this practical software application, Xu Bing has found a way of medially translating Chinese writing culture into the pictographic age of global digital communication' (Mersmann 2019: 72). In this context, one might say Xu is hypertranslating verbal signs into non-verbal signs. This is especially evident in an offshoot of *Book from the Ground*, namely the digital program WordMagick. The program affords an interactive dimension to the work by translating words into signs, allowing users to write and share their visualized stories across language boundaries (Lee 2015: 119).

Xu Bing's other projects, too, bring forth the hypertranslational in all their transmodal mutability. *The Genetics of Reading Image* (2021–2022) is an exhibition that reminds one of *Book from the Ground* in its extensive use of emojis and memes. It supplies traditional knowledge with new elements and thus provides a better understanding of traditional and contemporary cultures. Images and pictures show the continuity of communication 'in the context of the cyberpunk and space age ... Today, our daily lives are deeply intertwined with the use of cell phones, which serve as our portable libraries and museums. As soon as we turn them on, our first instinct is to read the signs they present to us'.[15]

Artificial Intelligence Infinite Film (AI-IF) Project (2017-), as the name suggests, involves artificial systems in film production, with the audience inputting their preferred film genre and customizing the narrative plot by entering keywords or sentences. This AI-generated movie experiments with the future possibilities of AI film. It transcends human creation and works with AI scientists 'to develop a real-time feature film production artificial intelligence system that involves no human production personnel (directors, screenwriters, photographers, or actors, etc.) ... Its concept emerges from human biases, including narrow emotional perspectives, political and economic interests that breed greed and immorality, as well as limitations in knowledge that impose restrictions'.[16] *Square Word Calligraphy* (1994) is especially engaging here because Xu designs a calligraphic system in which English words resemble Chinese characters. He invents a new hybrid of language by intertwining Chinese calligraphy and English letters. He uses it in such works as *Poem*

---

[15] https://www.xubing.com/.
[16] https://www.xubing.com/.

Stone Chairs (2019). *Square Word Calligraphy* is different from *Book from the Sky* because it contains 'real' text. In this way, Xu introduces 'a novel Eastern art form into the Western cultural sphere. It transcends established notions of Chinese and English, reshaping perceptual norms and challenging the very foundation of cognition'.[17] Also relevant is *Monkeys Grasp for the Moon* (2001, 2008), where Xu Bing alludes to an ancient folktale and presents a series of monkeys formed out of word shapes: 'Each line in the shape is the word "monkey" in a different international language, including Hindi, Japanese, French, Spanish, Hebrew and English. These words are stylized to resemble monkeys themselves'.[18]

3.2 Antoni Muntadas

Antoni Muntadas uses translation in digital spaces to highlight the interaction among languages, (in)communication and cultural rewriting. As he himself argues, he translates into images what is now happening in the world. He works in parallel, not linearly, on projects that are at different stages and in different places. Many of his projects take place over a long period of time, like, for example, *On Translation*, a multi-sited, multilingual, and multimodal series starting in 1995, which today includes sixty-nine works and is still open. He calls his artworks 'projects', because those projects are constantly moving, never close, in progress, collaborative, and open to input. In fact, he encourages public involvement. *On Subjectivity* (1978), for instance, introduced the idea of participation as central to his work and analyses how information is disseminated, received and interpreted. Muntadas questions how images are rewritten, what mechanisms are used to construct information and how we are influenced by what the networks chose for us. He is interested in 'reading between the lines' as the title of a 1979 installation warns us, which means looking beyond, deeper, than the printed words, analysing how we complete, interpret, and translate thinking, knowledge, and information. His projects have different levels of interpretation which grow out of social, perceptual, and cultural differences. He encourages his audience to have their own interpretations, but also to raise questions and discourage absolute values. The audience is part of the translated reality in which, according to the artist, we all live.

In *On Translation: On View* (2004), Muntadas demonstrates that public art is a way of questioning the context in which the viewer experiences that art. In this work, as in a hypertranslation, he assumes the role of the one who must rewrite

---

[17] https://www.xubing.com/.
[18] https://www.xubing.com/.

Figure 1 Antoni Muntadas's *On Translation: On View*. Courtesy of Antoni Muntadas.

the work of art in a given social space. In all the projects of the *On Translation* series, Muntadas presents himself as a multimedia artist for whom space is a very important element, because space and spaces are incorporated and absorbed in his projects. *On Translation: On View* (Figure 1) was created in Japan and produced in New York. The work is a seven-minute film of an anonymous space, one of those non-places so characteristic of globalization (Augé 1992/1995). When we listen to the film, there are background noises that in a certain sense recall John Cage's *4'33"*. As Modesta di Paola observes, the panoramic perspective is recorded 'in a sequence shot, giving the feeling of being reproduced by a surveillance camera. An undetermined eye, therefore seeing while being unseen the movement of people and things. In turn, the viewer that watches the video feels confused trying to understand what people are watching'.[19]

Muntadas creates a non-linguistic translation that could be considered visual hypertranslation because he plays with ambiguity and the unexpected while forcing us to participate, as he does in all of his works. As in so many of his other projects, this participation leads to an open interpretation at different levels, depending on a variety of social, cultural, and political issues. Each viewer becomes a visual hyper-translator, whom Muntadas invites to not only make his/her own rewritings but also to ask difficult questions that have no univocal

---

[19] https://interartive.org/2016/08/antoni-muntadas-2.

answers. The viewer must thus interact, be co-author, and interrelate different senses if the message is to be understood. That is why one of his artworks is titled *Warning: Perception Requires Involvement* (2000).

On Translation: On View is 'a kind of translation of what we see/hear/feel'.[20] It is a kind of Foucaultian panopticon that arises in an anonymous non-space, which forces us to wonder about who these people are, what they do, and where they are. It is not only a paradox 'of "what" is observed and "who" observes, but it is also effective to reflect on the "how" and "why" the observation takes place while waiting for what might happen that maybe it will never happen'.[21] This non-space reminds us that Muntadas creates all of his projects from the idea that we live in a translated world where the processes of transcription and translation are related to the processes of perception and information. In this sense, *On Translation: On View* hyper-translates looking and waiting as contemporary rituals. This resonates with hypertranslation, since Muntadas

> makes mediality a conceptual art practice by treating translational technologies themselves as the grist or filters of medium. Where other artists have focused on revealing how art 'translates' the mediatization of natural or social environments, Muntadas takes the media environment itself, along with its second-order transposition to other media systems, as subject to translation. Muntadas archives images, sounds, language, and text in his installations, monitoring and resetting their context parameters. (Apter 2006: 204–205)

On Translation: The Internet Project (1997) (part of the documenta X exhibition in Kassel, Germany) addresses issues of transformation of meaning and interpretation throughout the process of translation. It demonstrates that language is never static, constantly flowing and changing according to different ideologies and world views, and is thus a prime example of hypertranslation. This is a participatory exercise modelled on the telephone game. *The Internet Project* developed the translation of one English sentence ('Communication systems provide the possibility of developing a better understanding between people: in which language?') through twenty-three different languages. The English sentence is sent to a Japanese station to be translated into Japanese, and then to Germany for translation from Japanese to German. After that, it is forwarded to Pakistan to be translated again. The process goes on like this through a total of twenty different sites until the circle is closed with a translation from Russian back into English. From the last station, the process begins again and goes on indefinitely. So, Muntadas proposes that there be

---

[20] https://interartive.org/2016/08/antoni-muntadas-2.
[21] https://interartive.org/2016/08/antoni-muntadas-2.

a constant flow of changing language in translation.[22] It is important to bear in mind that in 1997

> there were limitations on character sets, and the inability of e-mail programs and Web interfaces to read non-Roman characters meant that participants had to default to older technologies – fax and the postal system – with, for example, messages containing Japanese, Arabic, and Cyrillic characters eventually scanned and published as picture files. Hence the cautionary note for viewers of the äda'web site: 'Due to computer network and cross-platform transmission [translation], the project may require a little willing suspension of disbelief' (www.adaweb.com/influx/muntadas). (Muntadas in Raley 2016: 127)

As a participating translator in the process, Raley (2016: 128) highlights the bureaucratic difficulties recorded in e-mail communications as well as 'the intrinsically situated aspect of any translational act, particularly including the differential relationship each translator has to the temporal dimensions of work: to national holidays, vacations, working hours, schedules, lag'. Raley goes on to highlight that the invisible labour of the translators foregrounds the asymmetry between agents and languages. Such a foregrounding makes one think of 'the fallacies of equivalence and commensurability, the notion that a metaphysical sameness underlies all human languages' (Raley 2016: 129).

As mentioned earlier, the translations also change according to the different world views. The sentence went round the circle of translators twice, so that in the end there were two versions of the phrase in each language and three in English, which is the first and last language in which it appears. Like the 'broken telephone' or the surrealists' 'exquisite corpse', the production of the text is effected through 'feedback loops' that generate an unpredictable and collaborative result. If we follow the line of translations correlatively, the first thing we notice is that the most significant changes in the meaning of the phrase occur when it comes into contact with Eastern languages with a sign system different from those with Greek-Latin roots. For example, Japanese seems to translate English 'communication systems' well, no doubt due to the intense contact that Japan has had with Western culture during the twentieth century, and in fact there do not seem to be any problems with the translation of the Japanese term into German, which gives the word 'mitteilungssystem'. The problem arises in the translation of this term into Korean, or in the Spanish translation of the Korean word so that, instead of 'communication systems', the result in Spanish (from Bolivia, by the way) is 'sistemas de transmitir las intenciones' [systems to transmit intentions]. From this point on, the meaning

---

[22] http://adaweb.walkerart.org/influx/muntadas/project.html.

of the original phrase falls apart, while its original semantic content is left unsaid: it seems that 'communication systems' do not provide the expected 'better understanding between people'.[23] The last translation of the English phrase at the beginning of the third round is far removed from the original: 'At the end of it all, we are left with practically only an echo of the meaning of the original phrase, and what really comes out explicitly in the last version is an annoying overlapping of points of view, which we can only attribute to the subjectivity of each of the translators'.[24]

Muntadas extended his experimentation with translation as medium to the realm of software and computational linguistics. As explained by Emily Apter, the work resembles

> a coil or helix, suggesting a 3-D diagram of the Tower of Babel, contained a single phrase rendered in twenty two languages, each of which could be audio-accessed depending on where the viewer clicked on the spiral. In this way, the translation engine of machine translation programs (like Babelfish and Altavista) was in effect 'seen,' or at least visualized as an interface, much like the human translators in the translation booths in the earlier works. Where non-Roman alphabets could not be entered into the translation program (because the engine did not recognize their characters), they were used to fabricate multilingual collage. Pieces of language, arrayed in polyglot graffiti walls, drew attention to the visual dimension of the translational medium. (Apter 2006: 205–206)

Muntadas uses language in translation as a medium that makes visible 'invisible zoning laws of circulation and mobility' (Apter 2013: 106). He deconstructs the possibility of a universal translation through digital media. The concept of physical space is very important to him in order to highlight the negative consequences of globalization and Western capitalism. His art intends to interfere in the public space, but also to influence and bother the private space. For Muntadas, the approach is very different when the project is going to be seen in a protected space like a museum or a gallery to when it is being seen in the streets of a city, on television or on the internet. Each space needs a specific kind of negotiation, but it also leads to different signifiers in different cultures. He performs all over the world, in a wide range of territories, towns and cities, and networks, from Beijing to New York, passing through Barcelona or Tijuana. But Muntadas also reflects on communication through digital territories. For many years now, Muntadas has also shown an interest in digital space, what

---

[23] https://tecnologiasliterarias.wordpress.com/category/2-antoni-muntadas-artista-investigador-y-cientifico-creativo/26-on-translation-the-internet-project/.

[24] https://tecnologiasliterarias.wordpress.com/category/2-antoni-muntadas-artista-investigador-y-cientifico-creativo/26-on-translation-the-internet-project/.

Appadurai calls *technoscape*: 'the global configuration, also ever fluid, of technology, and of the fact that technology, both high and low, now moves at high speeds across various kinds of previously impervious boundaries' (Appadurai 1990: 297): for example, in *Media Sites/Media Monuments* (1981) Muntadas points out spaces where relevant political and social events have taken place and then have been forgotten.

The Internet Project exemplifies how communication is always open, heteroglossic, in constant movement, never fixed. In this sense, *The Internet Project* can be seen as an example of hypertranslation rather than experiential translation. Muntadas's projects point at the growing homogenization of our global digital culture, which is a way in which power translates reality, and urges us to think of those in-between spaces, like the digital space, which are so dangerous for power, since they are spaces of separation but may turn (or not) into spaces of connection, transgression, change, dislocation, and disruption of accepted narratives of utopia:

> Media appear physically as neutral carriers of pure discourse are manipulated by invisible systems. Within the context of current political struggle, both dominant groups and those in opposition articulate and disseminate information through their understanding and manipulation of these 'invisible mechanisms'. Via media campaigns, posters, radio, and television, power is enforced not so much by the gun but by sound and image. (Muntadas in Danzker 2012: 60)

Another project concerned with technoscapes is *The File Room* (1994), whose main theme is censorship from the point of view of the collaboration of spectators through digital space, thus showing how what has traditionally been private becomes public. *The File Room* took place in the Chicago Cultural Center, a building dating back to 1897 which was formerly home to the largest network of libraries in the city. For this reason, Muntadas locates his work in a space which is halfway between the public space of the street and the specialized space of the museum. But also in the internet space, because it is a project made up, above all, of archives referring to censorship, and through computer networks is how they can best be consulted:[25] *The File Room* is a Kafkan space, barely lit, with 7 computers, 138 metal filing cabinets and 552 glass cases. From the computers, spectators can access censorship cases but also, using a computer located in the centre of the room, input their own examples of censorship.

Muntadas's projects make us aware of liminal space, a space more explicitly understood as 'a site of transitivity, a point of entry into another zone . . . a space

---

[25] http://fileroom.aaup.uic.edu/FileRoom/documents/homepage.html.

of opening, unfolding, or becoming figured in the form of the Deleuzian nomad living in the intermezzo, ever deterritorializing without reterritorialization' (Downey et al. 2018: xi). Soja's third space, 'the space where all places are, capable of being seen from every angle, each standing clear; but also a secret and conjectured object, filled with illusions and allusions, a space that is common to all of us yet never able to be completely seen and understood' (Soja 1996: 56). Muntadas approaches reality from 'unbelonging', and thus turns into art projects Bhabha's reflections on border lives, when he argues that in-between spaces 'provide the terrain for elaborating strategies of selfhood that initiate new signs of identity and innovative sites of collaboration, and contestation' (Bhabha 1994: 1–2). The interstitial spaces of borders 'open a possibility of cultural hybridity that entertains difference without an assumed or imposed hierarchy' (Bhabha 1994: 4).

Muntadas's projects aim to become spaces of negotiation and interrogation, multifaceted spaces of transition that contest binarisms and boundaries in order to question status quo worldviews and to show that globalization blurs our perception of diversity and therefore, far from leading to a reduction of walls, makes some spaces more equal than others. For power, having control over space is essential. That is why the spaces shown in these projects are mapped by power as texts which are written asymmetrically depending on a very diverse series of political and economic interests. According to Muntadas, the Internet is a tool with which spheres for questions and communication generated by interactivity can be created, not just between artists but also between creators – in a broad sense – and observers. (More recently, however, Muntadas's optimistic view of the Internet has shifted. He now adopts a more critical stance toward the Internet which, "while interpreting and transmitting, also takes control of the medium and manipulates information – it does not translate reality but falsifies it with fake news, and in other cases leaves that reality in the hands of consumerists, thus annulling individual opinion [influencers, for example]" [personal communication, 30 June 2024]). For him, translation is no longer a mere substitution of words but a transformation between or among codes.

4 Memes, Intersemioticity, and Experientiality

Hypertranslation as a perspective on translation is motivated by trends in translation theory and practice focusing on materiality and multimodality.[26]

---

[26] See Tanasescu & Tanasescu (2023), where the authors explore the impact of digital infrastructures on the materiality of translated literary texts. A further development and more complex perspective can be found in Tanasescu (2024a) in which the author explains the communicative

This section briefly discusses three interrelated themes, with an eye on distinguishing hypertranslation from affiliate concepts. As we will see in the next section, hypertranslation, while drawing on current interests in the heterogenous modes and media of translation, lifts the conception of translation beyond the level of practice and captures the ephemerality and networked character of virtual communication.

4.1 Memes

The meme is a fundamental concept that underpins hypertranslation. A meme is the motif, concept, or structure underlying any piece of communication that makes it 'tick'.[27] The term, coined by Richard Dawkins as the cultural counterpart of biological genes, originally references any distinctive and recallable unit of sociocultural life (e.g., fashion statements, architectural styles, and image templates) with a potential to be distributed across timespaces by 'leaping from brain to brain via a process which, *in the broad sense, can be called imitation*' (Dawkins 2006: 192; emphasis added). This idea of memic distribution as an imitative process has been used in the study of Internet memes. Here, memes are dynamic, iterable units of communication disseminated on new media platforms. They are 'multimodal signs in which images and texts are combined [and] would typically enable intense resemiotization ... in that original signs are altered in various ways, *generically germane* – a kind of "substrate" recognizability would be maintained – but situationally adjusted and altered so as to produce very different communicative effects' (Varis & Blommaert 2015: 36; emphasis added). The latter definition raises the concept of *resemiotization*, which in turn is related to *entextualization*.

Entextualization refers to the process whereby a sign is extracted in part or in whole from its original context of inscription (decontextualization) and planted into a different textual environment (recontextualization) (Bauman & Briggs 1990), and this de- and re-contextualization always leads to a change in 'meaning outcomes' (Varis & Blommaert 2015: 36). Thus, sharing a Facebook or Twitter post takes a piece of communication from one textual and participatory framework (the latter comprising 'friends' and 'followers') and recycles it in another, leading to different uptakes of varying degrees of impact. For example, a quote

---

model that 'forms the bedrock of literary translation and advocates for incorporating medium-awareness and relationality to our understanding of literary translation in the digital age'.

[27] Compare: Roland Barthes's *seme*, referring to 'the unit of the signifier' from a semantic perspective (Barthes 1970/1974: 17); for example, the scene of a party held in a luxurious mansion in a rich neighbourhood indicates the seme Wealth. Also compare *texteme*, which refers to 'any linguistic or textual feature (ranging in size from a single sound to an entire textual segment) which takes on a special functional significance in a given literary text (or context)' (Shuttleworth & Cowrie 2014: 168); examples include rhyming words, key repetitions and puns.

from a famous philosophy classic will have a different emanation of meaning in a Twitter group formed around new age counselling than in one formed around entrepreneurship: the same quote may be appropriated as an inspirational source of spiritual awareness in the former and as a pragmatic resource for business strategizing in the latter. And when this same piece of text leaps from one medial environment to another (e.g., from the page of a book to a post on Twitter), it is subject to resemiotization, 'the process by means of which every "repetition" of a sign involves an entirely new set of contextualization conditions and thus results in an entirely "new" semiotic process, allowing new semiotic modes and resources to be involved in the repetition process' (Varis & Blommaert 2015: 36). Examples include the stock templates Keep Calm and XXX and I Love XXX, circulated across memorabilia, advertisements, and online platforms, with different affective-rhetorical motivations and outcomes depending on what XXX is.

The important point for us is that the basic unit of hypertranslation is not the word but the meme, the conceptual or structural economy of a text; and that Internet memes 'repeat' or replicate themselves randomly via resemiotization, resulting in a tension between creative transformation and generic identity. As we all know, memes are not simply 'copying units' but translated cultural units which incorporate many layers and asymmetrical variations, post topical comments out of the 'original' author which modify its content and sometimes localize it. They are multimodal rewritings, semiotic units that reconfigure, rewrite, and translate contemporary issues based on an original (an image, a film, a song, and a text) which the target audience recognizes. In fact, internet memes are rhizomatic, and may function as cues of membership or serve as a sort of creative and social glue that bonds members of a community together.

We can now begin to reconfigure the linear and primarily linguistic filiation of meaning between a start text and a translated text into the lateral or oblique extension of memes, which distribute centrifugally along diverse pathways via non-trivial (performative) acts of translation. This ensues in a translational network of nodal points (linguistic, non-linguistic, or multimodal forms), 'viscously' related to each other by way of their substrate recognisability. Hypertranslation references the summation of the 'interobjective' or intertextual spaces arising from this network.

4.2 Intersemioticity to Transmodality

Because hypertranslation entails an unboundedness with respect to the boundary between not just languages but also modes and media, intersemioticity sits at its core. There is already a vast volume of research on intersemiotic translation, with transcreation (à la de Campos) being a critical source of inspiration. As is well-established, the term's classic definition traces to Jakobson (1959/2012: 127): 'an interpretation of verbal signs by means of signs of nonverbal sign systems', otherwise called 'transmutation'. This presupposes a movement from one distinct mode to another; and on this initial definition at least, the vector of movement is unidirectional – from verbal to non-verbal, not vice versa – clearly placing a premium on verbal-linguistic signs as the source of meaning.

In reality, a mode or medium almost never operates alone, such that any single piece of communication must be heterogeneously constituted. For instance, Instagram posts often entextualize Tik Tok clips, which in turn comprise music, dancing, lip-synching, posturing, and so on. In this regard, hypertranslation has a more sophisticated take on the conventional idea of intersemiotic translation. If no text is strictly monomodal, it makes more sense to think of intersemiotic translation as a transition from one *repertoire* – an already differentiated continuum of resources from plural languages, modes, and media – to another. Since there is no one-to-one correspondence between modes here, directionality loses its relevance altogether.

On this point we might have recourse to the idea of transmodality from applied linguistics, which 'index[es] the simultaneous co-presence and co-reliance of language and other semiotic resources in meaning-making, affording each equal weight' (Hawkins 2018: 64). The term underscores the entanglements and intersections between modes in the course of 'shap[ing] meaning in multimodal artifacts and communications' (p. 64). It brings forth the imperative to transcend the familiar distinctions between modes and to think in terms of semiotic resources, which are 'embedded and given meaning *within the specific assemblage, and within trajectories of time and space, continuously shifting and re-shaping in their contexts and mobility*' (p. 64; emphasis added).

The *trans-* in transmodalities pushes beyond the *inter-* in intersemiotic translation by signalling a breaching of conceptual as well as disciplinary boundaries traditionally imposed on modes and media. Riding on this, the hyper- in hypertranslation takes intersemiotic translation from a *crisscrossing* of medial borders – which in a way also reifies their existence – to a *transcending* of the very notion of such borders within a complex flow-and-flux of semiotic production.

4.3 Experientiality

A significant development along this vein is the concept of experientiality, as championed by a group of scholars from the AHRC-funded Experiential

Translation Network (ETN),[28] which derives from the Intersemiotic Translation and Cultural Literacy Group under the European Science Foundation's Cultural Literacy in Europe initiative.[29] Dovetailing into the material turn in translation studies (Bennett 2022) as well as cognitive translation studies (Alves & Jakobsen 2021), experiential translation spotlights the embedded, embodied, and extended nature of translation (Risku & Rogl 2021), embracing the rearticulation of aesthetic ideas between and beyond semiotic borders of every variety (see Campbell & Vidal 2019). In focus here is the multisensory *experientiality* of translating derived from an *experimentalism* with respect to the deployment of signs. Experiential translation takes the locus of translating out of a discrete text, language, mode, or medium, and locates it within the translator's body, more specifically their matrix of senses.

Experiential translation puts a different spin on intersemiotic translation, the latter now seen as taking place *within* the multisensory, phenomenological experience of a text through which 'the translator (artist or performer) offers its embodiment in a different medium'. Thus understood, intersemiotic translation

> is facilitated by perceiving and experiencing non-verbal media through visual, auditory and other sensory channels, for example through dance or sculpture. Instead of focusing on the translation of sense or meaning, *the translator effectively plays the role of mediator in an experiential process that allows the recipient (viewer, listener, reader or participant) to re-create the sense (or semios) of the source artefact for him or herself.* This holistic approach recognizes that there are multiple possible versions of both source and target texts and this can help mitigate the biases and preconceptions a static, intra-semiotic translation can sometimes introduce.[30]

Strongly aesthetic in orientation, experiential translation pursues a radical resemiotization of a given work by bringing the aspect of materiality into high relief. As an example, Figure 2 shows a translation of Leroy Anderson's whimsical musical piece *The Typewriter* by África Vidal Claramonte and Sofía Lacasta Millera (both members of ETN) – into a concrete poem. Anderson's musical piece is characterized by the distinctive type-and-bell sounds of a typewriter punctuating a rapid cascade of notes played by stringed instruments.[31] Vidal and Lacasta's rationalization of their translation strategy, which demonstrates the calculated and creative synergies between sounds, texts, and images, is worth quoting in full:

---

[28] https://experientialtranslation.net.
[29] https://cleurope.eu/activities/sigs/intersemiotic_translation/.
[30] https://cleurope.eu/activities/sigs/intersemiotic_translation/.
[31] www.youtube.com/watch?v=9OuKPtcYcZ0.

THE TYPEWRITER

TRANSLATED BY A.V.C. AND S.L.M.

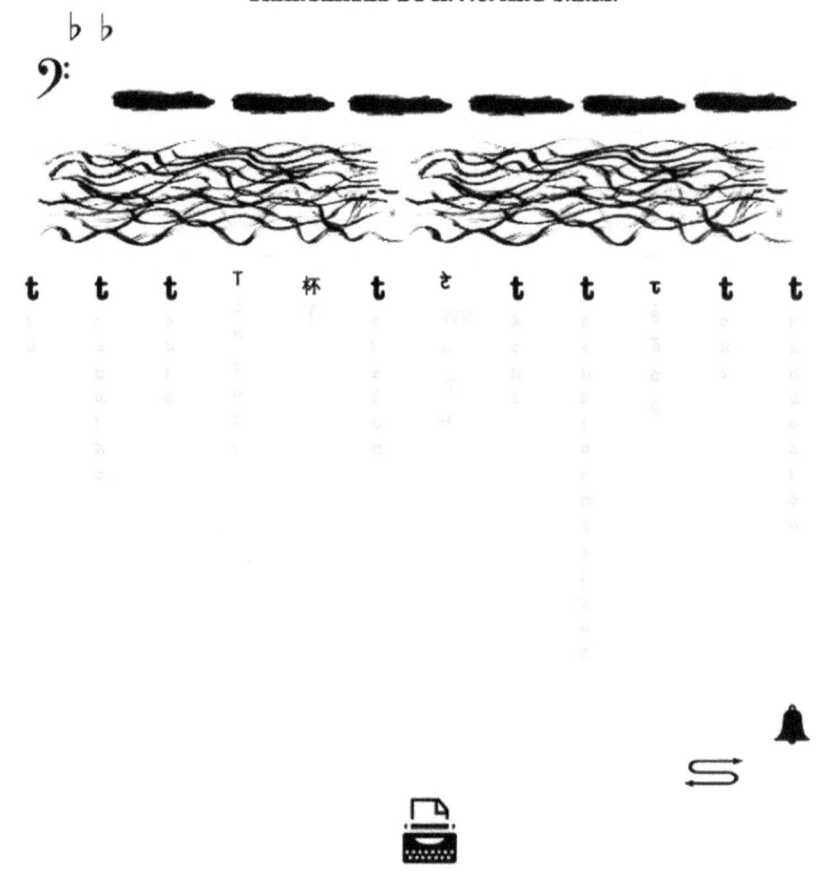

Figure 2 Experiential translation of Leroy Anderson's *The Typewriter*. Trans. África Vidal Claramonte and Sofía Lacasta Millera. Courtesy of the translators.

[J]ust as Anderson breaks the traditional elements of a concert hall by including an object which is not 'appropriate', we break down normative modes of syntax by also including signs and forms which are not part of a traditional poem. *Pitch* is translated into our poem through our use of the typewriter's traditional *font* in the title. *Timbre* is deconstructed by Anderson through the use of a 'new' musical instrument that uses noise and silence. This is translated into our poem through the use of *void spaces*. The particular timbre of the typewriter is also translated through the repetition of *sounds* such as the 't'. Anderson's *rhythmic patterns* are rewritten through the *visual distribution of words* throughout the page. *Strikethroughs* are also a way of translating the timbre of the musical instrument included by Anderson. We also translate the musical score into visual elements that include words in the traditional way, but also others such as *varied typography, punctuation marks, symbols and spaces*.[32] (Emphasis added)

Thus, the memes – the idiosyncratic elements – in Anderson's piece are rendered using a range of techniques appealing to verbal, visual, and auditory modalities simultaneously. Pitch is resemiotized as font type; timbre as empty space, sound, and typography (strikethroughs); and rhythm as visual arrangement of words. The concrete poem is furnished with other icons such as a bass cleft, two B flat signs and a bell, serving as surplus signs that nonetheless cohere with the musical meme. One also notes the curious presence of a Sinitic character and a South Asian script. Furthermore, Anderson's original and this experiential translation also reminds one of Steve McCaffery's *Carnival the First Panel* (1967–70), where we find the typewriter functioning 'as instrument of composition' (Rothenberg & Joris 1998: 822) before the days of computing. The poem becomes a site of carnivalesque where, beyond the poetry itself, the materiality of the book artefact becomes crucial to meaning-making: '*Carnival* was planned as an anti-book typographic environment motivated by a desire to expand the concrete text beyond the single page parameters of the majority of visual poems. Designed as a book with perforated pages [to be torn out & realigned in sequence], the book must be destroyed in order to "read" the piece' (Rothenberg & Joris 1998: 822).

A few more examples would suffice to illustrate the multisensory poetics of experiential translation. Guilherme Braga translates Saint Saëns's musical pastiche *Les tortues* into a poem, where the interplay between the poem's varying rhythmic patterns (the meme) is translated into alternations of disyllable-based and trisyllable-based lines. Ricarda Vidal translates Rimsky-Korsakoff's orchestral piece *Flight of the Bumblebee* into a multicoloured drawing by visualizing the frantic rhythms and repetitive motifs of the music (the meme) into a series of multicoloured visual transitions that appear to the viewer as frenzied, cyclical, and bewildering. Tricia Anderson and Gaia del Negro choreograph Akal Ki's ambient soundscape *Aukai* into dance movements where, for instance, the meme of musical tempo is resemiotized as the beat of walking, and the meme of pitch contrast is translated into the kinetics of small versus expansive movement.

In all these examples, translation is oblique in that it is impossible to speak of a mapping from the one text to the other. The notions of source text and target text become immaterial precisely because of the drastic transformation

---

[32] This and other examples of experiential translation were created in the workshop series Soundscapes: Translating from Music, organised by Karen Bennett in April 2022: https://soundscapestranslatingfrommusic.wordpress.com/gallery/.

in materiality. The translation output itself is semiotically heterogeneous and linguistically indeterminate, thus defying the conventional translation formula that goes from one delineated language, mode, and medium into another.

Another example of how hypertranslation deals with materiality can be found in the exhibition *The Weight of Words*, co-curated by Clare O'Dowd and Nick Thurston at the Henry Moore Institute (Leeds, 7 July–23 November 2023). The work features

> an international and intergenerational mix of contemporary artists and writers, all of whom pursue poetry through sculptural means. Ranging in tone from the humorous to the haunting, expressing everything from direct quotations to the unsayable, the works on show entangle the two art forms by compounding the three-dimensional and linguistic qualities of words. Together, they reveal what can happen to languages and our experiences of them when sculptural interests in weight, materiality, form and arrangement are charged by a poetic impulse to see words take on depth and presence. The shift between the two-dimensional experience of written language and the three-dimensional experience of sculpture requires a different way of looking and reading that happens physically, across space and time ... Many of the works do not feature words at all, and instead are focused on presenting the unsayable; giving meaning to experiences that cannot be adequately conveyed through words alone.[33]

The materiality of words hypertranslates their meaning into different media through dust, mirrored metal, a tongue torn in two directions, crouching calligraphy, a twelve-step interrogation of strangers, and many other different ways of experiencing and translating meaning. Poetry and sculpture intermingle using entangled modes.[34]

What experiential translation does instead is to resemiotize one multimodal cluster of signs, through the translator's sensory intervention, into an assemblage comprising a different mix of signifying resources. The implication, as suggested above, is that translation resides not so much in a product or process as it is embodied within the translator's sensory – not hermeneutic – interpretation. It is, as África Vidal Claramonte (2022: 9) aptly puts it, 'a heterotopic activity that exists between different spaces and epistemological times ... that crosses, not only all contemporary arts, from music, painting, and dance to literature, but also every moment of our life, from birth to death ... a way of exploring our relationship with language(s) through its physical and sensory effects on our bodies'.

---

[33] https://henry-moore.org/press/the-weight-of-words/.
[34] For an overview of the materiality of language in art, see Lopez 2013.

It is here that experiential translation resonates with hypertranslation where translation is conceived as a dynamic flow-and-flux in the *space-between*. Yet, experiential translation differs from hypertranslation in several respects. First, it places a strong premium on the translator's embodied agency; with hypertranslation, as we will see, agency is distributed among human and non-human actants. Second, experiential translation is invested in the physical (largely non-digital) outcomes of translation and has a strong aesthetic agenda, as evidenced in ETN's art exhibitions and projects; hypertranslation, on the other hand, foregrounds virtual networks rather than individual performance and, as a corollary, considers translation output as fleeting data. Third, it positions itself as 'a method of creation and communication, as a method for learning and teaching, collaboration and participation'[35]; hypertranslation, as repeatedly emphasized, references not a discrete method of translating, but a field of mobile relations; it is a *siteless site* for semiotic networking.

5 Hyperreality: When the Body Translates

The *hyper-* prefix, in virtue of its longstanding association with digital space, typically invokes virtual communication, and it is in this domain that hypertranslation best demonstrates its theoretical viability. Yet hypertranslation is not simply moving professional interlingual services into cyberspace (cf. O'Hagan 2001). *Hyper-* is less about going *between* one language, mode, and medium and another than it is about going *beyond* these semiotic categories as such. Eschewing the etymological sense of translation – transference from one point to another – it transcends, transgresses, and transforms (cf. the idea of translanguaging: Li 2018).

5.1 John Cage

An example is John Cage's compositions, which let chance,[36] as in the *I Ching*, 'control' creativity. Cage started using digital technology and computer programming in 1984 and presented his first computer-assisted works in 1988 in a series of lectures at Harvard University in 1988. He first used a program, Mesolist, written by Jim Rosenberg, which mechanically performed Cage's treatment of texts through his mesostics. Cage also used other programs, such as his assistant Andrew Culver's program IC, which emulates the calculations of the *I Ching* (Funkhouser 2007: 64).

---

[35] https://experientialtranslation.net/about-2/network/.
[36] John Cayley (2019: 44–47) analyses some of Cage's 'Songs for C.W.' (and Carol Richards' translations of those mesostics into French) in terms of chance operations and dissonances. See also Caley (2018a: 86, 224).

I-VI is a clear example of what Cage writes in *A Year from Monday* (1969: 50): 'What we need is a computer that isn't labour-saving but which increases the work for us to do, that puns (this is McLuhan's idea) as well as Joyce revealing bridges (this is Brown's idea) where we thought there weren't any, turns us (my idea) not "on" but into artists'.[37] Cage used chance operations as a form of Buddhist/anarchist non-interference and 'a means ... of silencing the ego so that the rest of the world has a chance to enter into the ego's own experience' (Cage in Rothenberg & Joris 1998: 114). Cage's collaged *Diary* or *Song with Electronics* can be seen as examples of hypertranslations, since they are palimpsests derived from other writings whereas the poems he wrote for Merce Cunnigham exemplify his mesostics, where the verticality of the message is central (Rothenberg & Joris 1998: 114).

John Cage's multimodal, multi-site, polycentric work is an example of what we are calling hypertranslation because it deconstructs boundaries and goes beyond any kind of border between disciplines. His poems, his musical silence, include noise, objects, and movement; all tones resound in an all in all, entangled and infinite, never ending, creation of meanings through non-linguistic media. His messages are disrupted by subversive noise. The borders of music are dissolved. Cage's music and poetry trespass the conventional limits of any discipline and, instead, offer ambivalence and equivocality. It highlights difference rather than sameness, and pervasiveness rather than opposition.

5.2 Multisensory Art

Experiments with synaesthesia and augmented reality exemplify this transgressive potential of hyper- with respect to experiential translation, discussed in the previous section. Here, multisensory experiences are *translated impressions* 'formed by specific events where someone has carefully crafted the sensory elements in them' (Velasco & Obrist 2020: 26). For example, in lieu of taking someone to a field of roses, one could create an impression of such a field, say, in a room, by appealing to multiple sensations associated with roses, including the visual (using bright red as a dominant colour), the olfactory (evoking sweet, earthy scents using a mixture of natural substances), and the tactile (manipulating the room's temperature and lighting and using carefully positioned air coolers to create the ambience of spring). A field of roses becomes literally *sensational* even in the absence of the real thing.

Consider how we might reanalyze a multisensory art exhibition hypertranslationally; and how, conversely, the intersections between sensorial or virtual

---

[37] Other examples are Jim Rosenberg's *Instagrams* and John Cayley's HyperCard innovations (Funkhouser 2007; Seiça 2021). See also Hayles (2002) and Grigar & O'Sullivan (2021).

technologies and the human senses inform a hyper-view of translation. The exhibition we have in mind is Tate Sensorium, held at the Tate Britain in 26 August–4 October 2015. This is an award-winning immersive art experience featuring four paintings that are not merely looked at, but also listened to, tasted, felt, and smelled. As an example, one of the exhibits on display was John Latham's *Full Stop* (1961), which paints a large black circle in the middle of a plain canvas. Tate Britain describes the painting as follows:

> The spot was created by repeated action with a spray gun, its curve delineated using weighted sheets of newspaper cut to the correct shape and, as a result, traces of rectangular forms are faintly visible outside the circumference. The circle's edges are blurred, particularly on the left side where a sprinkling of tiny and slightly larger dots emerge from the dense black of the large spot ... the blurred edges of the spot and the slight halos around some of the larger dots at its circumference recall a solar eclipse, a black hole or the negative of photographs of light reflecting off planets in the dark galaxy.[38]

Latham's is not just a piece of abstract visual composition; its memes are hypertranslated into a sonic-tactile experience. The viewer is surrounded by a soundscape, via speakers, created to conjure an aurality that transmutes the tension between the positive (black paint) and negative space (the rest of the canvas). This sound-image speaks to the memic image in the painting of 'a solar eclipse, a black hole or the negative of photographs of light reflecting off planets in the dark galaxy'. Intriguingly, a contactless mid-air haptic system, which uses the properties of sound waves to create mid-air pressure, is installed to transmit a tactile sensation on the viewer's hands, namely a sense of circular motion that modulates in radius and intensity. The latter synaesthetically resonates with the visual theme of the painting 'where a sprinkling of tiny and slightly larger dots emerge from the dense black of the large spot' on its edges. The touch-pattern of 'roundness' felt on the viewer's hand alternately eases into a rain-like pattern, which reverberates with the tactility suggested by Latham's 'repeated action [of painting the black circle] with a spray gun'.[39]

It is important to note that this hypertranslation of Latham's painting in the form of sensorial augmentation does not unfold independently of the painting itself. The visitor experiences the augmented painting holistically; the visuality, aurality, and tactility do not manifest as separate modules but in orchestration, hence dissolving any clear sense of a source or target text. This simultaneous orchestration of different modes, each speaking to a different

---

[38] www.tate.org.uk/art/artworks/latham-full-stop-t11968.
[39] This description is adapted from Velasco & Obrist (2020: 8).

meme of the painting, is integral to the artwork as it is experienced by the Tate Sensorium visitors, where they could experience 'sounds and savours in conjunction with viewing selected artworks, for example, sampling chocolate and listening to urban noise while looking at a stark Francis Bacon painting' (Classen 2017: 135).

Whereas in experiential translation, the translator's body is still positioned outside a source text and expresses itself in a separate target outcome (e.g., from a poem to a musical score), hypertranslation transgresses this inside–outside boundary – *the viewer's body encapsulates both the start text and the translation through embodying a transmodal, synaesthetic experience*. In other words, the work as it is experienced embeds its own translation, rendering irrelevant the idea of translation as an extrinsic outcome of a procedure undertaken in respect of a prior work.

Examples of art as hypertranslation can be found in many other sites of contemporary art. It is true that the museum in the West has 'a long and troubling history' (Sturge 2014: 431). Museums shape knowledge (Sleeper-Smith 2009) and therefore have power (Bennett 2018). They have prescribed how bodies should behave and be positioned within that space: art museums and exhibitions have imposed 'different modalities of looking, walking, hearing, sitting and talking (but less frequently, touching, tasting or smelling) from their emergence in the eighteenth century' (Leahy 2012: 3).

Furthermore, the role of the senses in museums – in all *senses* of the word – is also beginning to change. And this is especially relevant for our purposes. Museums have traditionally been spaces only related to the sense of sight,[40] places of pure spectatorship where unique works of art were kept behind glass cases to prevent being touched while standing at the correct distance from the artwork. Whereas the museums of the seventeenth and eighteenth centuries allowed visitors to handle objects, the nineteenth century expected museum visitors to remain detached from the objects on display and in modernity the importance of the sight increased. This was because touch 'was no longer understood to provide any important information about the world. The important thing was to *see*' (Classen 2005/2020: 260; see also Classen & Howes 2006).

However, museums are beginning to see art through all the senses and so they are more attractive, interactive, and engaging for contemporary visitors.

---

[40] For a discussion of the senses in museums, see also Howes and Classen 2014: 17–36. Furthermore, in Chapter 3 of this book, the authors take a most interesting journey from the Middle Ages to the present day to describe how the emphasis on different senses in different cultures has resulted in social ordering. In this way, they emphasize the politics of perception. See also Classen 2017.

Because the nature of contemporary art is changing, museums, at least some museums, curate exhibitions in which art is no longer conceived as a realm of pure visuality but as a process to be experienced with all our senses: 'Artists no longer confine themselves to the kinds of works that can be appreciated by gazing at them from behind a rope or painted line on a museum floor. They are creating art which must be moved through, handled, played, smelled and even eaten' (Classen 2017: 115). Art experienced through the senses may even have a healing power (Cowan et al. 2020).

The rehabilitation of touch is a salient trend in this new museology (Howes 2014: 259. See also Classen & Howes 2006; Gadoua 2014). Furthermore, the 'rehabilitation of touch has in turn created a more receptive environment for the (re)introduction of other senses traditionally classified as "base" – in contrast to the "higher," "aesthetic," "distal," "intellectual" senses of sight and hearing – such that smell and taste are now being actively solicited instead of censored' (Howes 2014: 260). Classen gives several examples: the installation in the Toledo Museum, entitled *Harmonic Motion* and hand-crocheted by Toshiko Horiuchi MacAdam and Charles MacAdam, the *Please Touch* exhibition held at the British Museum in 1983, the 2005 Victoria & Albert Museum interactive exhibition entitled *Touch Me*, scent in Monet's paintings in an exhibition at the Denver Art Museum (2015), the exhibition of olfactory art held at the Tinguely Museum in Basel (2015), and *Atmosphere* (FoFA Gallery, Concordia University, Montreal, Canada. January 2011), an exhibition which can be described as 'both an act of translation and performance; translating but not representing the intersensorial mingling that is the focus of the ethnographic accounts while performing this sensory information through a lived enactment' (Salter 2015: 188).

Also worth mentioning is *Food: Bigger than the Plate* (Victoria and Albert Museum 2019), a bold interactive exhibition including over seventy projects by artists and designers working with chefs, farmers, scientists, and local communities that invite visitors to participate in gastronomic experiments, from urban farming to synthetic meat. Co-curators Catherine Flood and May Rosenthal Sloan (2019) remind visitors that food is one of the most powerful tools through which we shape the world we live in, from how we create society, culture and pleasure to how we determine our relationship with the natural world. *Food: Bigger than the Plate* takes visitors 'on a sensory journey through the food cycle, from compost to table, [and] poses questions about how the collective choices we make can lead to a more sustainable, just and delicious food future in unexpected and playful ways'.[41]

---

[41] www.vam.ac.uk/articles/about-the-exhibition-food-bigger-than-the-plate.

What is most interesting is precisely that the exhibition uses not only intellect but all the senses to convey information to the visitor. This information is also related to current issues, such as products from local communities, the use of compost to cultivate organic products that reuse waste, 'or cutting-edge technology in farming through a working version of the MIT' Food Computer. *Food: Bigger than the Plate* is also in line with the now classic Food Studies, which regard food as far more than mere nourishment for human beings. Over the years, food has become a singular way of understanding the world. It involves cultural processes of representation, and concerns culture, identity, and religion, as well as many other issues. Not surprisingly, translation studies has also adopted this way of understanding food. Food is a relatively recent research line in translation studies that had its most important exponent in a special issue of *The Translator* (2015, Vol. 21, Issue 3), followed by another in *Terminology* (2017, Vol. 23, Issue 1). Other more recent references include an issue of *Perspectives* (2024) and the Routledge Studies in Global Food Translation Book series. What is striking is that all these publications view food as an object that translates "history, identity, power relations, art, policy, the environment, and so on" (Desjardins 2015: 258). Food transmits messages, "provides information and, ultimately, signifies" (Chiaro & Rossato 2015: 240).

In this exhibition, food translates through all the senses, because as previously mentioned, many contemporary museums have already begun to encourage visitors to use their body as well as all their senses, not only sight. In this exhibition the visitor finds edible water bottles, a pair of plastic toilets, an empty vending machine, glasses frames made from coffee grinds, buttons made of McCain's oven French fries, or vases comprised of cow's blood. Visitors can talk to plants through new technologies, learn how brands have changed the way we understand food through visual storytelling and come across cheese made from human bacteria and mushrooms grown from coffee grounds taken from the Victoria and Albert Cafe.

More than translation, food is here hypertranslation because in this food exhibition, in the same way as in many other exhibitions, the senses become entangled. The content not only translates in a linear way but also in multiple transversal ways, like a rhizome that interrelates all the senses. Furthermore, the artwork in the exhibition is not only interdisciplinary and research-based, but also uses a variety of media that take us from urban farming to gastronomic experiments and synthetic meat. This type of artwork embarks us on a multisensory journey that allows viewers to travel from composting, farming, and translating to cooking, and eating. In the exhibition catalogue, the curators write that in these works, food provides 'a nexus for creative experiments' (Flood & Sloan 2019: 11). Through this multisensory journey, where diverse media are interrelated and intertwined, these works also hypertranslate because they raise questions, alternative options, and critical stances against the current food system of the consumer society. It is about tasting with your hands, in a creative and open way.

This leads us to a tangible (Ciribuco & O'Connor 2022) hypertranslation that through the materiality of food-related objects shows that 'looking at materiality can enable a multilayered conceptualization of the processes and cultural significance unleashed by this movement. Attention to tangible translation can thus help translation scholars better grasp the totality of translation and its relationality' (Ciribuco & O'Connor 2022: 5). This tangible and material approach to translation broadens the definition of translation and shows that translating today is 'a model in which the linguistic aspect, while important, does not coincide with the whole idea of translation and careful attention is paid to the geographical, material, and political migrancy of knowledge, people, texts, and objects' (Bertacco 2023: 119). The sensory entanglement proposed by the artwork in *Food: Bigger than the Plate* causes viewers to rewrite with their whole body, enabling them 'to explore translation from a non-linguistic angle' (Bertacco 2023: 118). They permit us to understand translation as an experiential process that transcends language, and which occurs with our whole body and our five (or more) senses, through the materiality of objects.

What this exhibition has in common with hypertranslation is the fact that it is interactive. At one point, the visitors encounter a long table in the middle of the gallery where they are invited to make their own food and eat it. But first, at the Loci Food Lab (2014–2019), created by the Center for Genomic Gastronomy as a traveling food stand, the visitor makes their selection on a Tablet and algorithms create a customized snack for that person. In *Food: Bigger than the Plate* food is shared, reinterpreted, and misunderstood – and in so doing, it is hypertranslated. In this context, hypertranslating means confronting a complex interplay of language(s), sensory experiences, and socio-cultural norms, to be rendered 'in a different language or mode of communication . . . the strategies for translating . . . food relate to different semiotic systems, but also to relations of power' (Ciribuco 2021: 9).

5.3 Virtual/Augmented Reality as Hypertranslation

As another illustration, consider the digitally augmented food experience Meta Cookie. This illusion-based, pseudo-gustatory setup (Narumi et al. 2011) uses an AR head-mounted display (HMD) set, two cameras, and an air-pump spraying device capable of emitting different scents. A user wearing the HMD holds a plain cookie, whose physical properties are registered by the headset and transmuted into code. The user then chooses a flavour from a range of options (chocolate, maple, strawberry, etc.), which prompts the air-pump device to emit the smell of the selected flavour and the HMD to superimpose the relevant colour (dark brown, pink, etc.) onto the image of the plain cookie as seen through its lens. The system also detects the shifting distance between the cookie and the user's face, increasing the concentration of the smell as the user brings the cookie nearer to his or her mouth (Velasco & Obrist 2020: 41–42).

With this multisensory manipulation, the user has the illusion of tasting different cookie flavours even though all the cookies are in fact plain. Translation in this case lies within the illusion itself, which is superimposed on and thus unseparated from the plain cookies – the original 'text', if you will. Whereas the Latham example engages auditory and tactile sensations, the Meta Cookie example uses sophisticated technologies to transform the user's visual, olfactory, and gustatory perception of an object-text. As it were, the plain cookie is translated, the latter process transpiring within the user's experience of a single complex artefact. More precisely, the transmodal integration of sight, smell, and taste (Narumi et al. 2011) *translates the cookie into a multisensory spectre of itself*. This demonstrates the user's mediated agency in a translational experience driven by AR, thus amplifying the Cyborgian idea of the human-machine interface – an essential feature of Web 5.0. Again, as with the Latham example and in contrast with experiential translation, translation does not occur as an operation distinct from the user's experience of the source – the painting and the cookie. Instead, the object is spatially and temporally congruent (Velasco & Obrist 2020: 24) with its multisensory transmutation, creating a rich embodied experience that emanates from, conflates with, and goes beyond an artefact or text. This very transcendence of the perceived borders between interfacing, intersecting, or mutually transformative entities (objects, languages, modes, and media) is hypertranslational.

Such hypertranslational experiences as Meta Cookie are not necessarily restricted to the laboratory. Pokémon GO, a smartphone game wildly popular in the mid-2010s, is an example of hypertranslation experienced in everyday settings. The game makes use of AR, together with smartphone cameras and location trackers, to overlay players' real world with virtual imagery, enabling players to simultaneously traverse physical and digital landscapes in pursuit of animated creatures. What ensues is a palimpsestic hyperreality where the player enacts *an embodied liminality* within the superimposed space of virtual and non-virtual realms. As scientists have described it, the game 'leverages AR to introduce *virtual objects* at fixed and dynamic locations that *translate* through the app interface *to incentives in the real world* that potentially influence users' route and mode choices' (Guo et al. 2022: 395; emphasis added).

Apple Vision Pro represents the recent milestone in respect of VR and AR, with immense implications for how we engage translation both in the more pragmatic sense (e.g., subtitles) and as a heuristic for understanding the altered temporalities and spatialities of trans-platform communications. Powered by Apple's visionOS, described as an 'intuitive spatial user interface, and magical input system that users navigate with their eyes, hands, and voice'.[42] This reference to our multisensory faculties takes us back to the theme of embodiment; but the revolutionary potential of Apple Vision Pro lies more specifically in the way it alters the timespace dynamic of communicating. It augments the real-world space by superimposing a virtual canvas on which the user can transit seamlessly across different platforms as well as between the real and virtual realms, thus (in an uncanny way) reviving translation in its etymological meaning. Storytelling is said to be changed forever by the Apple Immersive Video function, which uses spatial audio and 3D 8 K video technologies to create three-dimensional interactive experiences. Fictional characters and voices can be carried across – translated – the interface into a hybrid zone where the boundary between real and virtual becomes porous. Language barriers are rendered immaterial by means of translation applications, such as Live Captions, which translate conversations from FaceTime as well as streaming content into subtitles *in real-time*. With this, translating is no longer a discrete practice but occurs in tandem with and as part of the multimodal package of communication. This blows up the traditional conception of translation premised on a spatial and temporal gap (however small) between a source and a target; and it is in this breaching of the source-target distance and the real-virtual divide that translation in the age of AI can be said to be *hyper-ed*. The figure of Babel Fish in the *Hitchhiker's Guide to the Galaxy*, it seems, is no longer the stuff of fantasy.

6 Apropos of AI: Hypertranslation as a Semiotic Condition

Exponential advancements in material technologies have fundamentally altered the way we manage and perceive texts. The medium on which a work is communicated (e.g., codex vs. smartphone) impacts 'how a reader encounters the work', and 'by changing *how* the work means, such a move alters *what* it means' (Hayles 2003: 264). It is worth noting that N. Katherine Hayles (2003: 263) proposed more than two decades ago that 'the transformation of a print

---

[42] www.apple.com/newsroom/2024/06/apple-vision-pro-arrives-in-new-countries-and-regions-beginning-june-28/.

document into an electronic text [be seen] as a form of translation'. Taking as her case study the *Blake Archive,* she argues that 'even small differences in materiality potentially affect meaning, so they have gone to a great deal of trouble to compile not only different works but extant copies of the same work. Yet these copies are visually rendered on screen using a technology that differs far more in its materiality from print than the print copies do from one another ... Translating the words on a scroll into a codex book, for example, radically alters how a reader encounters the work; by changing *how* the work means, such a move alters *what* it means' (Hayles 2003: 264).

The permeation of computational media in the printing industry has clear implications for this understanding of translation. Hayles (2021) makes this point by ruminating the difference between the first edition of a classic work and its digital reprint on-demand:

> Musing, you hold two books, one in your left hand, the other in your right. The left-hand book is a first edition of William Faulkner's classic novel *The Sound and the Fury* (1929), for which you paid a staggeringly extravagant sum at a rare-book dealer. The right-hand book is a copy of the same novel that you bought on Amazon for a tiny fraction of that cost. Although you may not know it, the right-hand book was printed by CreateSpace, a digital publishing platform, at a nearby location to ensure you would receive it the next day. The bindings of course are different, but other than the colophon and publication date, all the words in both texts are the same. What do the differences matter, you think, except to a bibliophile like you, who prizes the aura of a first edition? Both are print books, aren't they? (Hayles 2021: 1)

6.1 John Cayley

The increasing facility with which signs can be transmuted across languages, modes, and media has rendered communication ever more translational. Many examples come to mind – Eduardo Kac's *Genesis* (1998/1999), Michael Kargl's *on translation* (2008/2009), among others (see Raley 2009). But an especially relevant case is John Cayley's *translation* (2004) (Figure 3), developed from an earlier work, *overboard* – which may be easier to look at than to read and is impossible to classify as either visual art or literary writing. Cayley explains that these works are underlined by texts arranged with line and stanza breaks and that each of the resulting verses may be floating, sinking, or surfacing, three material states on the screen whose names are highly suggestive. The writing produced renders the surface as complex, manifold, shifting; and the drifting metaphors suggest that we might think of this 'as like the surface of the sea, deformed by interfering wave patterns. The texts are particular patterns of ever-shifting wave-deformed surfaces. Where the surfaces touch, literal

Hypertranslation 49

```
                          réalité ne se forme que dans la memoire
                          les fleurs qu'on me montre aujourd'hui
                          pour la première fois
                          re we semblent pas
                          de vraies fleurs

                          mil dem erwähnten verhältnis
                          der sprache als dam von medien
                          verschiedener dichte ist
                          die übersetxbarkeit de sprachen
                          ineinander gegeben

                          un na la setis enejl qes
                          en me marert  o pund d'ora rjyièra
                          uû if y aurejl
                          d'eosc  paaoz nvwpheec
                          angujcce poj emigra darc    awuun

                          fa lrebostior pencuurt
                          ar fes treverser  bec  ontinus
                          ba metamorprucac
                          ror bec re ionc apc  ajlec
                          be simjl lube at d  raccawblansa
```

Figure 3 John Cayley's *translation*. Courtesy of John Cayley.

writing appears. As waves rise and fall and where the surfaces no longer touch, writing disappears' (Cayley 2018a: 87).

In these works, we find Cayley's digital technique of transliteral morphing (see Cayley 2021: 106), 'a computational procedure that algorithmically morphs, letter by letter, from a source text to a target text' (Hayles 2008: 145). In *overboard,* the surfaces of the text are deformed by functions relating to legibility and the 'wave-pattern' of a verse. For example, in a 'surfacing' state, 'literal points (points on the surface where letters may appear) will tend to "rise" and touch the screenic surface of visibility such that it will spell out the underlying given text'; whereas in a 'sinking' state, they 'recede' from the surface of visibility. And in a 'floating' state they are 'algorithmically transformed so as to appear on the visible surface in an alternate literal form, producing a quasi-legibility, a linguistic shimmering on the screenic reading surface' (Cayley 2018a: 87).

In *translation*, Cayley deploys similar algorithms but introduces further complexities, 'demonstrating the contention that the surface of writing may be arbitrarily complex ... In *translation,* the wave-patterns of textual surfaces may be deformed by literal functions relating different texts to one another, specifically texts in different languages. If a text floats or sinks in one language, it may surface in another. As they run and perform, pieces from the *overboard* and *translation* series are what they appear to be – everchanging, ambient manifestations of writing on complex surfaces. Neither *overboard* nor *translation* can be read or appreciated as flatland literary broadsheets' (Cayley 2018a: 87–88). *Translation* is a time-based work of digital poetry with generative music by Giles Perring. What we see is a black screen gradually replaced by fragments of images of paper pages containing passages, including Benjamins's 'On Language as Such and on the Language of Man'. These passages 'undergo an interactive algorithmic translation process, moving from computational, visual and textual realms, blurring boundaries between English, French, and German. The translation process is never finished, never fixed'.[43]

Another example is Cayley's *Indra's Net* pieces which employ generative algorithms and semialeatory processes. Here,

> the composition of the algorithm is seen as an integral if normally invisible part of the composition of the piece. One of the unique facilities offered by the computer in this context is the ability to set up a feedback loop. 'Experimental' texts can be generated and the results reviewed quickly and painlessly enough to allow the processes to be modified and improved. Once distributed, the pieces 'run' and generate text for a reader. The reader can interact but does not choose pathways between words directly in the way that she might choose a pathway through the spaces of hypertext fiction. However in my most recent distributed piece, readers can alter the work itself (irreversibly), collecting generated lines or phrases for themselves and adding them to the hidden given text so that eventually their selections come to dominate the generative process. The reader's copy may then reach a state of chaotic stability, strangely attracted to one particular modulated reading of the original seed text. (Cayley in Rothenberg & Joris 1998: 828)

A crucial development in this respect is the interplay between the algorithmic and the translational. Algorithmic translations, Raley (2016: 134) observes, 'offer models of critical engagement with the new linguistic doxa – resituating the technical within the cultural and manifestly reintroducing the aesthetic into the predominant terrain of commercial transaction'. Generative AI (GenAI) has taken this to unprecedented heights. Since the inception of Chat-GPT in November 2022, a plethora of GenAI applications driven by large learning models (LLMs) have mushroomed in the market, enabling users to convert linguistic text into code, sound, image, PowerPoint infographics, or other formations of linguistic text – all on the seat of their pants and at stunning speeds. Much of this is mediated by algorithms largely inaccessible to users, drawing on the voluminous, invisible ocean of bits and bytes floating in the digital universe. What Raley calls algorithmic translation has assumed a new

---

[43] https://jacket2.org/commentary/kac-cayley-and-kargl-translation. For an analysis of Cayley's *translation* see Hayles 2008: 145–55. See also Cayley 2015, 2018b, 2021.

6.2 Eric Zboya

prominence in content and information generation in mundane undertakings both personal and professional.[44]

An example of algorithmic translation is Eric Zboya's *un coup de dés jamais n'abolira le hasard: translations* (2018), his hypertranslational treatment of a titular poem by Stéphane Mallarmé (Figure 4). Mallarmé's poem has been previously 'translated' through collaborative *livres d'artiste* by many artists

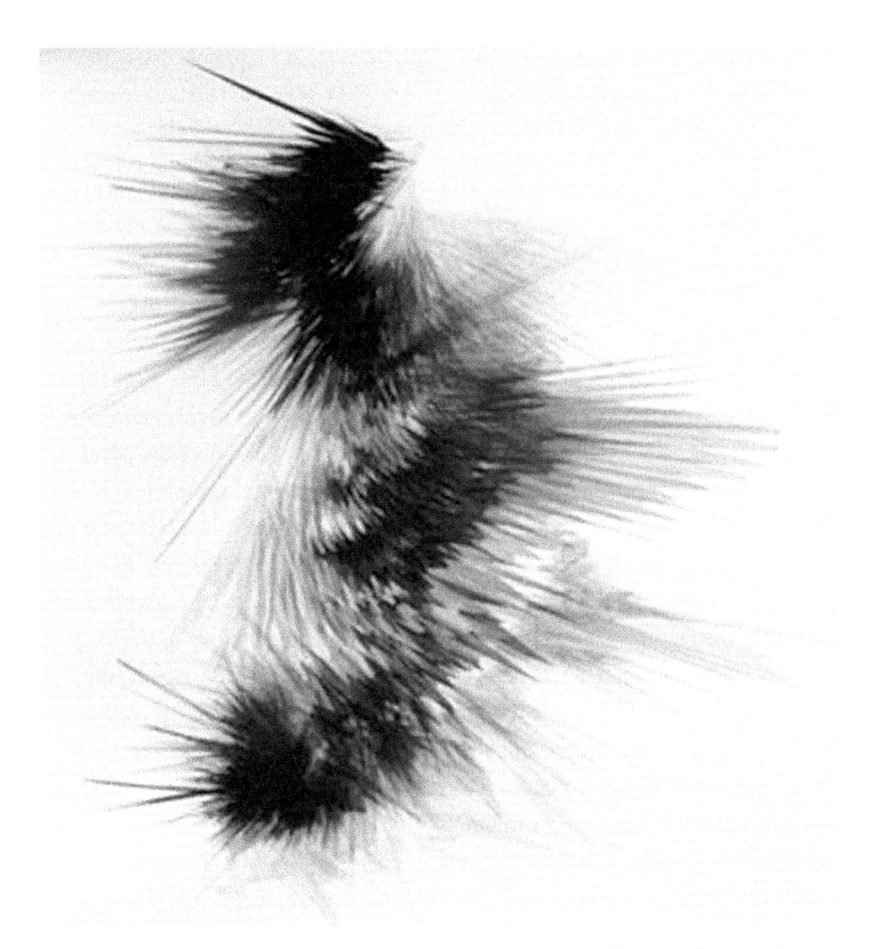

Figure 4 Eric Zboya's *un coup de dés jamais n'abolira le hasard: translations*. Courtesy of Eric Zboya.

---

[44] An excellent book on algorithmic translation including many examples of experimental and experiential translations in different media is Lily Robert-Foley (2024). Also interesting are her own experiments with language and different types of unconventional ways of reading in *graphemachine* (2013) and *Jiji* (2016).

who have produced dialogical renditions of Mallarmé, thus, among others, Marcel Broodthaers in his *Un coup de dés jamais n'abolira le hasard: Image* (1969); Guido Molinari in *aMeTrica n'ABOOlira* (1968); and Michalis Pichler in *Un Coup de Dés Jamais N'Abolira le Hasard: Sculpture* (2008). But Zboya's approach is different, as he tells Christiane Bök in an interview:

> Even though Marcel Broodthaers, Guido Molinari, and Michalis Pichler use different techniques to exhibit the spatial themes of dimensionality in *Un Coup de Dés*, all of these translators share a common approach, in that they all eliminate the referential text from the page. Broodthaers, for example, renders each line of text as a proportional series of black rectangles, all of which project like shadows through the translucent pages of the book, appearing gradually into view, then fading away, with each turn of the page. Molinari, likewise, replaces the lines of text with rectangles, except that, in his case, he employs a palette of bright colour to help delineate these spaces more vibrantly within the depths of the page. Pichler also takes this idea of erasure to an entirely new level by literally excising the lines of text, through the use of a laser, so that what remains is only a series of negative spaces, or 'anti-spaces,' which almost act as dimensional doorways into the other pages of the book.[45]

As Zboya states on his website, he showcases the 'dimensional potentiality' in Mallarmé's text through a computer-generated process he calls *Algorithmic Translation*. With the aid of graphic imaging software, this highly unique process transforms each letter, each mark of punctuation, each individual pixel into big bang bursts of frozen sound that propagate like cosmic sculptures through the space of the page. Zboya explains to Bök that he visits Ji Lee's website and takes from there the typefont he invented, a '3D-font' called Univers Revolved free for everyone to use. He takes the characters he needs, reduces them in size and places the on the space of the page, based upon the positions of the original text. Zboya argues that particular font gives each letter a tangible quality, a concrete depth. He generates a three-dimensional projection by recreating *Un Coup de Dés* on the computer and by transferring the image over to Photoshop. And then he creates two identical images of the text which he superimposes skewing 'one of them slightly to either the right or the left: the greater the horizontal displacement, the greater the illusion that the text either extrudes off the page or recedes deeper into the page'. In that way he manages to create a dynamic structure which makes the reader plunge into the page and at the same time 'literally showcases the notion of textual transcendence, since every word almost appears to ascend from the surface of the page into the space above it – (very cool . . .)'.[46] Significantly, Zboya explains in the same interview

---

[45] www.poetryfoundation.org/harriet-books/2010/04/the-higher-dimensions-of-the-poem-part-1.
[46] www.poetryfoundation.org/harriet-books/2010/04/the-higher-dimensions-of-the-poem-part-2.

Hypertranslation 53

how he uses in his translation a form of algorithmic extrusion that speaks directly to our idea of *hyper-*:

> In a manner much like the anaglyphic projections, I first recreate *Un Coup de Dés* in its entirety on the computer, reproducing precisely all the typographical characteristics of the poem – and once the text has undergone this mimetic operation, I transfer the forgery over to a program for editing graphics, where I mutate the text three-dimensionally through a series of computations. I use an algorithm that extrudes each of the letters into a 3D-model, and then I repeat this process again and again upon the resulting imagery, transforming it into multiple 'dendrites' that spike off the shell of the page. I might note that each algorithmic translation of a page can never be recreated in exactly the same way twice, due to the seemingly aleatory function of the software during this mathematical transliteration.[47]

Using non-traditional strategies, Zboya translates Mallarmé through algorithmic translation. He collapses the original into mathematics and space, scattering amongst his sculpture's fragments of Mallarmé's original phrases. He turns Mallarmé's text into virtual swirling sculptures in constant movement generated by algorithms. Zboya's texts are non-linear entities. He achieves this by turning each letter into an abstract image. But what is also relevant is that his texts mutate in unexpected ways, never following a previous pattern, because the program uses a randomization function which never generates the same image from the same input:

> In keeping both with the title (*Un Coup de Dés Jamais N'Abolira le Hasard*) and the poem's last line (*Toute pensée émet un Coup de Dés*), no run of the program ever abolishes chance, and every input (thought) generates a roll of the dice. Zboya's artist book presents more than these graphic, constellation-like translations of the text. Literally shadowing the right-reading English translation of the title is the French text set in reverse. Drawing the reader closer to the synaesthesia promoted by Mallarmé, Valéry and, before them, Baudelaire, the contrast of black (**English**) and gray (hcnerF) echoes the tonality of the algorithmically translated images; the reversed letters of the French emphasize the physical reversing that occurs when printing text; and the movement from the original hcnerF to the translated **English** urges the 'mind's ear' to play along with the mind's eye. The choice to print everything on the same highly textured Rives Design, Brilliant White, enlists hand and eye in support of a synaesthetic equation of text, page and image.[48]

---

[47] www.poetryfoundation.org/harriet-books/2010/04/the-higher-dimensions-of-the-poem-part-2.
[48] https://books-on-books.com/2020/06/01/books-on-books-collection-eric-zboya/.

In this connection, Charles Bernstein's preface to Zboya is revealing. Somewhat in line with Tom Phillips's *A Humument*, the text is erased to create a new text. Only words selected by Zboya appear in black in their original position on the page. Zboya does something similar with his creative manipulation of the poem's English translation by Basil Cleveland – he also erases some lines and leaves others with the text of the translated poem.

For instance, *At the Heart of the Shipwreck,* Zboya's translation of the second page of Mallarmé's book, and the only named piece in Zboya's series, is a mathematical transformation/translation of the original, a direct computer-generated translation, or transformation, of the second recto/verso page from Mallarmé's original text:

> Since the crux of Mallarmé's poem centers on a shipwreck (to which the second recto/verso page refers), a shipwreck in which the text of the poem comes to represent the ship's debris floating about in a kind of ordered chaos, the image-text offers the reader-viewer a kind of hydrodynamic depiction of what the waves generated by a sinking ship might look like. I translated/transformed this recto/verso page many times while simultaneously experimenting with the computer program I use (Photoshop) to create these kinds of images. With the aid of this program, I eventually manufactured the image-text you now see (it could very well be the opposite in that the computer program manufactured the image with my assistance). (Zboya in Barwin 2013: n. p.)

Zboya displays this translation of Mallarmé in a rhizomatic style, that is, as a hypertranslation:

> I wanted to display the work by suspending the piece in the center of a room. Or, by suspending the piece in such a way that would allow for the reader-viewer to walk around it at 360 degrees so that he or she could gaze up the image-text at all angles, very much like a three dimensional object. I wanted to give the reader-viewer the impression that they are very much in the same spatial environment as the image-text itself... To help give the impression of dimensionality and an environment beyond the flat surface of the page. This is what Mallarmé was trying to get at with his typographical play – that a vastitude exists beyond the confines of the two-dimensional space of the page. This is a way that one might connect both works together – through the idea of textual spatiality (or, perhaps spatial textuality). (Zboya in Barwin 2013: n. p.)

Zboya's translation of Mallarmé is a transformation, a scattering of images across the pages through the exploration of made marks which vibrate, move, and open our imagination beyond the flat, static text into the multidimensional that is *translation 2.0*:

With *Shipwreck,* the final product is, in fact, not a language, but rather the visual end result of pixel reconstruction based on mathematical computations. I guess, in this sense, translation comes to mean the conversion, or transcendence, of one medium to another). This is my sole aim – to illustrate the idea that 'any form of language' can and should be used and experimented with in the act of creating and in the act of translating. Translation should not simply involve French to English or English to Chinese. It is time we broaden our minds, and our poetic processes and practices, into something more 2.0. (Zboya in Barwin 2013: n. p.)

6.3 Generative Artificial Intelligence

All of this is taken to yet another order of complexity by GenAI, which underscores hypertranslation as immanent to the instantaneous flows and transformations of resources across languages, modes, and media. Preliminary research has attested that GPT systems can generate translations of higher quality than neural machine translation systems as embodied by Google Translate and DeepL (see Lee 2023). As a model of communication, linearity à la Shannon-Weaver will be outmoded (if it has not already); rhizomes are now a central figure for beholding what is to come. In the terms developed in this study, communication will become increasingly hypertranslational as linguistic and non-linguistic resources transact and transform at impossible speeds across multiple platforms. Instead of correspondences between stable points of reference, communication takes place within floating assemblages of resources where proliferating nodes (or clusters of nodes) transmute spontaneously and iteratively into any number of other nodes, which in turn translate themselves into yet other nodes without regard to conventional boundaries.

A simple demonstration with AI applications suffices to capture the *hyper*-nature of translational processes in this context. Hypotenuse AI is an application that features among other functionalities an AI image generator enabling the user to create images any number of times and in any number of permutations by providing simple specifications in words. Offhand we pull out Ocean Vuong's poem 'Kissing in Vietnamese' and ask: how might Hypotenuse resemiotize the poem's memes by drawing on the vast sea of word-image collocations on the Internet by way of algorithms not privy to me and most other persons? The program allows us to type only 250 letters in the 'Describe your desired image' box at any one time, so we divided Vuong's 134-word poem into four stanzas. A number of parameters can be set to the specifications of our image with varying numbers of options under each parameter. At random, we chose 'photograph' under Type; 'gothic' under Aesthetic; 'calm/dark/cinematic lighting' under Mood and Lighting; and 'Cinema 4D/realism/by Van Gogh' "as if somewhere, a body is falling apart and flames are making their way back through the intricacies of a young boy's thigh, as if to walk out the door, your torso would dance from exit wounds."

Figure 5 A visual translation of Ocean Vuong's 'Kissing in Vietnamese' (second stanza). Created by the authors on Hypotenuse (free version).

under Artist or Style. For each stanza of the poem we type in, Hypotenuse offers four image options to choose from, and we can keep regenerating different combinations of memes for the same piece of text for any number of rounds. So there are any number of permutations and combinations of images with respect to even just one poem. Figure 5 shows our four options for the second stanza ('as if somewhere, a body is falling apart and flames are making their way back through the intricacies of a young boy's thigh, as if to walk out the door, your torso would dance from exit wounds'). Among these options, we can choose one (we favoured the one on the top-right). And by repeating the procedure for all four stanzas and juxtaposing the selected images, we created our DIY translation of Vuong's poem into a set of visuals.

This type of algorithmic translation with AI leads to a number of important observations germane to hypertranslation. First, it is fully ergodic: there is a game-like randomness to the process. In the Hypotenuse example, we exert a degree of agency in inputting the text to be visualized and hand-selecting our preferred image among the available options (discarding the rest). Our choice of images, influenced by many contingencies not least of which are our aesthetic disposition and intellectual proclivity, affects the visual narrative – consider the affective nuances among the four images in Figure 5. One might argue that this much is also true of intersemiotic and experiential translation. In an AI context, however, any intervention by oneself is inextricably caught up in an unfathomable web of algorithmic calculations, leading to unique and unpredictable pathways of translation. In this apparently intersemiotic translation, it is not just the boundary between word and image that is crossed but more crucially that between the human mind and the algorithmic matrix – the latter is where the prefix hyper- gains its valence against trans- and inter-. As with communication in superdiverse contexts (Cowley 2012; Pennycook 2018; Thibault 2011), translation in algorithmic contexts becomes *distributed, embedded, and extended* within a dialogical relation between human and machine bodies, organic and artificial intelligence (see Risku & Rogl 2021). This creates a new ecology where translational action is shaped by situated activity (e.g., our engagement with Hypotenuse) with 'situation-transcending meaning potentials' (Steffensen 2015: 109), namely the yet-to-become translations latent in AI algorithms.

The affordances of AI enable the iterability of algorithmic translation. To use the same example, we can repeat the process of word-image conversion any number of times until a suitable image series comes together. The outcomes of translation, with respect to AI, are transient in virtue of their potential *abundance* (an unlimited number of outcomes can be generated) and possible *redundance* (generated outcomes can be rejected by users at will). This fleetingness, this efficient and incessant to-and-fro, hither-and-thither between modes, takes the focus away from the final outcome of translation (even though they do exist materially) to the iterability of transmutation itself. The temporality of translation has now shifted: whereas hitherto translation encompasses a duration (however long or short) from source to target, algorithmic translation thrives on a cyclical involution where things happen at the click of a mouse only to begin again. And again.

Relatedly, algorithmic translation generates a plethora of textual relations where every click of a button can create a link or 'edge' (Latour 2005) connecting one node (a particular combination of memes) to several other nodes, each of which translates into disparate clusters of nodes ad infinitum. The resultant spatiality is that of a rhizomatic network that propagates itself through the recursive circulation and recycling of memes in cyberspace. Hypertranslation serves as a heuristic to capture this field of polycentric, multilinear relations where source, target, directionality, and authenticity are rendered indeterminate constructs set in perpetual flux and flow in virtual spaces. It constitutes a non-local, methodological field of semiosis where the translational (translation-as-methodology) becomes the *raison d'etre* that motivates the local production and perpetuation of signs within a constantly mutating digital ecology.

7 Conclusion

The advent of GenAI has fundamentally altered the game of contemporary communication. As regards translation, it no longer suffices to speak of the translator's creative intervention and critical agency – a theme with which translation studies scholars have been preoccupied since the early 1990s. It is now imperative that we push further: the human-machine interface in the age of AI has given rise to new textual practices to the effect that communication in general and translation in particular need to be conceived as *distributed and networked* across the boundaries between human and non-human actants, as well as between analogue and virtual modalities. With the increasing ubiquity of GenAI tools and continuing advancements in hyperreality technologies (think Apple's Vision Pro), we need to seriously ponder the impact of algorithms and the post-digital media on the conception of translation.

Hypertranslation offers a heuristic for cultural production as an iterative, indeterminate, multiplex, and embodied flux-and-flow of creative energies functioning as the nexus of knowledge regeneration. Because it is iterative, hypertranslation intersects with the idea of repetition. Artificial Intelligence and machine translation often focus on repetitive texts and generate output based on the patterning of previous versions of text. Iteration is linked to creativity. In fact, 'the challenge and question of repetition, iteration, and creativity are an exciting means by which to view translation – it is a disruptive concept that allows insights to emerge related to affective or experiential engagement with a text' (Mellinger 2024: viii). Our previous examples have shown how these layers of repetitions are an opportunity to challenge the stability of such concepts as authenticity and authorship 'that have been central to certain circles of reflection on the topic, further questioning what constitutes the "new" and how texts are created or constructed' (Mellinger 2024: viii). Hypertranslation as repetition is thus a process in constant motion and change. Repeating, like hypertranslating, is not reproduction, but rather the production, modification, and creation of something new. When something is repeated or hypertranslated, it becomes transfigured in a new context.

Hypertranslation speaks to a specific chronotope or timespace where the possibilities of instant transaction across languages, modes, and media lead to a virtualization of translating events into a field of mobile textual relations. In this sense, hypertranslation responds to a series of rhetorical questions posed by Clive Scott: 'What if translation is an adventure not in meaning but in readerly consciousness and the *experience* of language? What if reading is looked upon not as a process of interpreting, or extracting meaning from, text but as a process of existential/experiential self-coordination or self-orchestration? What if translation is not a test of comprehension but of the fruitfulness of our inability to comprehend?' (Scott 2019: 88). Hypertranslation plunges into an infinite multimedial space (see Tanasescu 2024a) that cannot be reduced to mere binaries. On the contrary, it involves territorializations, deterritorializations, and reterritorializations that imply constant transformations, insofar as its territory is Deleuzian, not a Euclidean or Kantian space with geometric coordinates. Hypertranslation approaches language as a mixture, 'a schizophrenic mélange, a Harlequin costume in which very different functions of language and distinct centers of power are played out, blurring what can be said and what can't be said; one function will be played off against the other, all the degrees of territoriality and relative deterritorialization will be played out' (Deleuze & Guattari 1975/1986: 19).

Hypertranslation encourages an ever-changing, reversible, connectable, non-hierarchical, and rhizomatic use of multimodal resources (including language), which are open to remapping, interconnection, and hybridization. The rhizome is a map, not a tracing. It can be torn, reversed, 'adapted to any kind of mounting, reworked by an individual, group or social formation. It can be ... constructed as a political action or as a mediation ... A map has multiple entryways, as opposed to the tracing, which always come back "to the same"' (Deleuze & Guattari 1980/1987: 12). Hypertranslation is anything but structuration: 'Unlike a structure, which is defined by a set of points and positions, with binary relations between the points and biunivocal relationships between the positions, the rhizome is made only of lines: lines of segmentarity and stratification as its dimensions, and the line of flight or deterritorialization as the maximum dimension after which the multiplicity undergoes metamorphosis' (Deleuze & Guattari 1980/1987: 21).

Hypertranslation is the queering of translation. It angles on any given text obliquely, seeking not a straight transmission of discursive meaning, but a centrifugal proliferation of multimodal potentialities. With hypertranslation the memes in a source text are but an initial stimulus to be articulated selectively and differentially by tapping into the repertoire of resources available and accessible to the translator (Lee 2022). Hence, hypertranslation always leads to *semiotic excess*, given that one set of memes can generate multiple iterations each offering a unique niche across different languages, modes, or media. Hypertranslation also generates affective canvases that appeal to our cognition, perceptions, and emotions, inviting us to translate sensuously through seeing, touching, hearing, smelling, and tasting. This mode of translation is a materially situated and 'critically engaged meaning making process, of exploring how experimenting with translation could invite the fixed forms of theory into a space of experimental possibilities' (Grass 2023: 2). With the ever-expanding affordances of AI, such experimental possibilities are heightened whereby virtual memes are entangled in complex loops of rhizomatic extension, circulation, recycling, recombination, and permutation, transcending artificial divides that have heretofore defined the semiotic order. Such is the crux of hypertranslation, which is set to become a fundamental condition of contemporary communication in Web 5.0 and beyond.

Bauman's (2007) prescient idea of liquid modernity is now coming into full view as GenAI continues to break every conceivable border and unsettle all things previously considered immutable or at least relatively stable. This is the time when translation needs to transgress its own discursive and disciplinary boundaries to reconceptualize itself as an experiential and experimental field of cultural and knowledge production transcending the borders between language and non-language, text and translation, as well as the real and the virtual. The Real, as it were, lies within the translational potentialities of multilinear and transmodal spaces sitting at the crossroads of the human and the posthuman. With the platformization of GenAI applications in contemporary communications, we suddenly find ourselves approaching the apex of liquid modernity – a sociopsychological condition that resonates with experiential and experimental views of translation that subvert conventional imaginaries of linear transference (Blumczynski 2023; Grass 2023; Lee 2022; Marais 2023; Robert-Foley 2024; Robinson 2022; Vidal 2022).

On this understanding, meaning is not static but plural and polyphonic; it is a complex palimpsest. They are stories within stories that take us to 'The Thousand and One Nights', in which Jorge Luis Borges asserts that layered stories create a strange effect, almost infinite, a sort of vertigo (Borges 1980/1984: 573), as in one of the seven Borgesian nights, where the mirror meets the labyrinth, where any point can connect with any other, and any voice with any other. Each word is a Library of Babel because it contains an infinite number of variations and multiple possibilities of meaning. And as in the Garden of Forking Paths, words capture moments with an infinite number of possible outcomes. Borges's mythical labyrinth, like hypertranslation, is infinite, made of twisting avenues, zigzagging paths, which make one think of a maze of mazes, of a sinuous, ever growing maze which would take in both past and future and would continue indefinitely, like the night in the middle of The Thousand and One Nights when Queen Scheherezade, through a magical mistake on the part of her copyist, started to tell the story of 'The Thousand and One Nights', with the risk of again arriving at the night upon which she will relate it, and thus on to infinity. As in 'The Thousand and One Nights', the story in *Seven Nights* in which Borges asserts that 'stories within stories create a strange effect, almost infinite, a sort of Vertigo' (Borges 1980/1984: 573). As in one of the seven Borgesian nights, hypertranslation is a space where the mirror meets the labyrinth. As if hypertranslation were a Borgesian universe, each word can be decomposed into an indefinite and perhaps infinite number of hexagonal galleries, an infinite palimpsest or a Borgesian set of facing mirrors (Borges 1999). Hypertranslation responds to Borges's Library of Babel, the library of all books, a haunting labyrinth composed of identical hexagonal galleries connected by staircases and staffed with imperfect librarians (Borges 1956/1986). The Library of Babel not only houses all books and languages but also the chronicle of their death. It contains both the true catalogue and the false catalogues. As observed by Borges in 'On William Beckford's *Vathek*' (1943), translation – which really is hypertranslation in our terms – *completes the original*. In 'The Homeric Versions', Borges further underscores the mobile and metamorphosing nature of translation, which offers differential perspectives on mutable facts. The concept of the 'definitive text' corresponds, he says, only to exhaustion. For Borges, translation is a process of creation. In 'The Homeric Versions' Borges affirms that in the translation of the classics, the first time is already the second time; an original is often (in a paradoxical turn of phrase) *unfaithful to its translation*, and so Borges states at the beginning of 'Two Ways to Translate' that he rejects the old adage, *traduttore, traditore*. Original and translation are concepts that are diluted with fuzzy boundaries, as in 'The Enigma of Edward Fitzgerald'. And finally, in 'Aladdin and the Wonderful Lamp' Borges argues that it does not matter that the original has never been found because the translator has as much right to add stories as the original storytellers:

> The most famous tale of *The Thousand and One Nights* is not found in the original version. It is the story of Aladdin and the magic lamp. It appears in Galland's version, and Burton searched in vain for an Arabic or Persian text. Some have suspected that Galland forged the tale. I think the word forged is unjust and malign. Galland had as much right to invent a story as did those *confabulatores nocturni*. Why shouldn't we suppose that after having translated so many tales, he wanted to invent one himself, and did? (Borges 1980/1984: 573)

Hypertranslation is a twenty-first-century Garden of Forking Paths, a heterogeneous, chaotic, contradictory, and incomplete space bifurcating in time, dizzily growing, and replete with alternatives which are not chosen one at the expense of the others but simultaneously. It creates various futures, that is, various timespaces which trigger others that will in their turn branch out and proliferate in other timespaces. It represents an ever-expansive network of diverging, converging, and parallel multiverses whose strands interface, coalesce, split, and repel each other, embracing every possibility including those yet to come into being.

These bizarre terrains in the Borgesian universe are now a reality, and very soon a commonplace, in the context of automations and algorithms, providing us with a visceral handle on hypertranslation. On a *hyper-* reading, thus, translation inflects itself into indefinite as well as infinite pathways, labyrinths, and galleries – with no beginnings and endings – in digital as well as non-digital spaces. Hypertranslation is not just about translation being non-linear; it is not just another construct in translation studies. It represents a paradigm of thinking about communication as a field of mobile relations between texts, one that will be of high relevance as we step into the age of GenAI.

Translation has for some time now pivoted its theoretical bearings from an instrumentalist model, which views translation as mere reproduction of pre-existing material, to a more open-ended model that rebrands translation as 'an interpretive act that inevitably varies source-text form, meaning, and effect according to intelligibilities and interests in the receiving culture' (Venuti 2019: 1). It is now well-recognized that translation is no longer a merely interlinguistic process 'limited to the quest for verbal equivalents across geographies and cultures'; it is rather an agentive practice with the potential to 'explain how things change through the modeling of the new upon the old' (Bennett 2023: 455). As a corollary the translator is no longer a servile figure. As Anne E. B. Coldiron states in the call for papers for a special issue of *PMLA* (May 2023), the time has passed when translations were valued for their faithfulness to an original and translators were considered servile copyists whose role was to remain invisible. In its new role, translation is dynamic, generative, and multipronged – an understanding that has been around in the field since the late 1980s and succinctly restated recently by Coldiron in the context of comparative literature:

> A common practical assumption is that a translation, if deemed good, will provide a fluent substitute and faithful transfer of content from the prior foreign texts or originals. Today most specialists in translation studies reject these common assumptions, as well as moralistic phrases like 'fidelity to the original' and concepts such as substitution and seamless transfer (inter alia). Instead, many translation studies specialists assume that translations do many more interesting things than replicate their prior foreign text(s) (an

impossibility anyway); that translation unsettles the idea of 'originality' and many other critical concepts ... the divergences between a translation and its prior text(s), like divergences among different translations of a work, are not problems but interpretive opportunities. (Coldiron 2023: 419)

Hypertranslation dovetails with this nuanced understanding of translation; but it also places a strong premium on how translation as a creative-critical undertaking imbricates itself within the crosslingual, intersemiotic, and transmedial networks of communication in the age of algorithms and deep learning. It imagines a Deleuzian map of heteroglossic and rhizomatic texts in which the (human) translator's voice intersects not only with that of the (human) author but also with that of artificially intelligent systems (switching among any number of roles) to create new synthetic voices. It expands the traditional definition of an 'original' text, conceiving the latter instead as 'a volatile compound that experiences continual textual reconfigurations' (Emmerich 2017: 2), as 'unfinished works riddled with variants, whose visual and material aspect many consider crucial to their modes of meaning' (Emmerich 2017: 161). The so-called original is here a participative and co-creative territory (Grass 2023: 22) where originals are as derivative in nature as translations (Emmerich 2017: 14). It is expected that these conceptions of the 'original' will gain new valencies in AI-mediated networks, compelling a *hyper-* perspective on translation that complicates the linearity of communication into spontaneous, rhizomatic ones.

Hypertranslation goes beyond experiential translation and creative adaptation insofar as it aims to be more than multi-authored, collaborative, and multimodal. It emphasizes the crossovers between art and literature, it underlines the importance of bodily sense, but goes beyond that. It is also cross-platform and post-digital. It aims to explore the impact of the new digital spaces on semiotic systems that go beyond the linguistic, and their influence on translation and on translators, an unresearched area in translation studies, although some scholars are beginning to overcome the status of mere imprint 'to become mediated "digital trace" suitable for digital (and even computational) examination' (Tanasescu 2024a). In line with this, hypertranslation proposes dynamic, never static, digital translational traces capable of including entangled interactions surrounding any signifying process. Hypertranslation opens new avenues for creative, rhizomatic approaches to the translation of new, infinite post-digital texts and non-texts in contemporary technoculture. Hypertranslation aims to keep up with the constant growth of platforms 'as new information is added every second, the permanent interaction between the human and the machine with consequences on both at the level of ever-changing identities and agency as well as the capacity to learn of an apparently unassuming information intermediary' (Tanasescu 2024a). Hypertranslation is crossbreeding, a mestization that embraces the unpredictable, interference, clash, transformation, errancy, multiplicity, and thus reshapes spaces and transforms each new meaning into an 'archipelago', in Édouard Glissant's sense, a translation that protects the diverse, that teaches us to think about evasive thinking, against dualistic systems; that leads us to the uncertain.[49] Thus, hypertranslation is close to Glissant's (1990/1997: 16) 'dialectics of rerouting, asserting, for example, political strength but, simultaneously, the rhizome of a multiple relationship with the Other'.

With hypertranslation, meaning is not just conveyed, but created; and not just created, but multiplied into diverse semiotic constellations, which instantaneously and iteratively transgress the boundaries between languages, modes, and media, as well as – significantly – the human/machine divide. In this regard, Borges (1956/1986) was never more accurate than when he stated that translation completes the original, broadens its meanings, opens up new interpretations, and asks questions that generate still other questions.

---

[49] 'L'art de traduire nous apprend la pensée de l'esquive, la pratique de la trace qui, contre les pensées de système, nous indique l'incertain, le menacé, lesquels convergent et nous renforcent. Oui, la traduction, art de l'approche et de l' effleurement, est une fréquentation de la trace. Contre l'absolue limitation des concepts de l' « Être », l'art de traduire amasse l' « étant ». Tracer dans les langues, c'est ramasser l'imprévisible du monde. Traduire ne revient pas à réduire à une transparence, ni bien entendu à conjoindre deux systèmes de transparence' (Glissant 1997: 28–29).

References

Aarseth, E. 1997. *Cybertext: Perspectives on Ergodic Literature*. Baltimore, MD: John Hopkins University Press.

Alves, F. & Jakobsen, A. L., eds. 2021. *The Routledge Handbook of Translation and Cognition*. London: Routledge.

Appadurai, A. 1990. Disjuncture and difference in the global economy. *Theory, Culture & Society* 7: 295–310.

Apter, E. 2006. *The Translation Zone: A New Comparative Literature*. New York: Princeton University Press.

Apter, E. 2013. *Against World Literature: On the Politics of Untranslatability*. London: Verso.

Augé, M. 1992/1995. *Non-Places: Introduction to an Anthropology of Supermodernity*. Trans. John Howe. London: Verso.

Badiou, A. 2010. *The Communist Hypothesis*. Trans. D. Macey & S. Corcoran. London: Verso.

Baker, M. & Saldanha, G., eds. 2019. *Routledge Encyclopedia of Translation Studies* (3rd ed.). London: Routledge.

Barthes, R. 1970/1974. *S/Z: An Essay*. Trans. Richard Miller. New York: Hill and Wang.

Barthes, R. 1975/1977. *Roland Barthes by Roland Barthes*. Trans. Richard Howard. Oakland, CA: University of California Press.

Barthes, R. 1984/1986. From work to text. In *The Rustle of Language*. Trans. R. Howard. New York: Farrar, Straus and Giroux, 56–64.

Barwin, G. 2013. Translation 2.0: *Eric* Zboya's at the heart of a shipwreck. *Jacket2* (22 September). https://jacket2.org/commentary/translation-20.

Batchelor, K. 2022. Translation as commentary: Paratext, hypertext and metatext. In M. Baker, ed., *Unsettling Translation: Studies in Honour of Theo Hermans*. London: Routledge, 48–61.

Bauman, Z. 2000. *Liquid Modernity*. Cambridge: Polity.

Bauman, Z. 2007. *Liquid Times: Living in an Age of Uncertainty*. Cambridge: Polity.

Bauman, R. & Briggs, C. L. 1990. Poetics and performance as critical perspectives on language and social life. *Annual Review of Anthropology* 19: 59–88.

Bennett, T. 2018. *Museums, Power, Knowledge: Selected Essays*. London: Routledge.

Bennett, K. 2022. Reflections on the material turn in translation studies and its intradisciplinary implications. In G. D. da Silva & M. Radicioni, eds.,

Recharting Territories: Intradisciplinarity in Translation Studies. Leuven: Leuven University Press, 49–73.

Bennett, K. 2023. Approaches to knowledge translation. In R. Meylaerts & K. Marais, eds., *The Routledge Handbook of Translation Theory and Concepts*. London: Routledge, 443–62.

Bertacco, Simona. 2023. Translation and migration. In P. Beattie, S. Bertacco, & T. Soldat-Jaffe, eds., *Time, Space, Matter in Translation*. London: Routledge, 118–35.

Bessa, A. S. & Cisneros, O., eds. 2007. *Novas: Selected writings. Haroldo de Campos*. Evanston, IL: Northwestern University Press.

Bhabha, H. 1994. *The Location of Culture*. London: Routledge.

Blommaert, J. 2015. Chronotopes, scales, and complexity in the study of language in society. *Annual Review of Anthropology* 44(1): 105–16.

Blumczynski, P. 2023. *Experiencing Translationality: Material and Metaphorical Journeys*. London: Routledge.

Bonito Oliva, A. 1990. *Art Talk: The Early 80s*. Boston, MA: Da Capo Press.

Borges, J. L. 1956/1986. *Ficciones*. Madrid: Alianza.

Borges, J. L. 1980/1984. The thousand and one nights. Trans. Eliot Weinberger. *The Georgia Review* 3 (Fall): 564–74.

Borges, J. L. 1989. La pesadilla. *Siete noches, Obras completas*. Barcelona: Emecé, 221–31.

Borges, J. L. 1999. *Collected Fictions*. Trans. Andrew Hurley. New York: Penguin.

Borowski, G. 2024. The metaphor of anthropophagy as a conceptual refraction in translation studies. *Translation and Interpreting Studies* 19(1): 21–32.

Braidotti, R. 2006. *Transpositions: On Nomadic Ethics*. Cambridge: Polity Press.

Brune, Krista. 2020. *Creative Transformations: Travels and Translations of Brazil in the Americas*. New York: SUNY Press.

Cage, J. 1969. *A Year from Monday*. Middletown, PA: Wesleyan University Press.

Campbell, M. & Vidal, R., eds. 2019. *Translating across Sensory and Linguistic Borders: Intersemiotic Journeys between Media*. London: Palgrave.

Campbell, M. & Vidal, R., eds. 2024. *The Experience of Translation: Materiality and Play in Experiential Translation*. London: Routledge.

Cayley, J. 2009. His books. In K. Spears., ed., *Tianshu: Passages in the Making of a Book*. London: Bernard Quaritch, 1–40.

Cayley, J. 2015. Untranslatability and readability. *Critical Multilingualism Studies* 3(1): 70–89.

Cayley, J. 2018a. *Grammalepsy: Essays on Digital Language Art*. London: Bloomsbury.

Cayley, J. 2018b. The advent of aurature and the end of (electronic) literature. In J. Tabbi, ed., *The Bloomsbury Handbook of Electronic Literature*. London: Bloomsbury, 73–94.

Cayley, J. 2019. The translation of process. In N. urovi ová, P. Petro, & L. Terando, eds., *At Translation's Edge*. New Brunswick, NJ: Rutgers University Press, 31–59.

Cayley, J. 2021. [Mirroring] events at the sense horizon: Translation over time. In M. Reynolds, ed., *Prismatic Translation*. Cambridge: Legenda, 96–118.

Chiaro, D. & Rossato, L. 2015. Introduction: Food and translation, translation and food. *The Translator* 21(3): 237–43.

Ciribuco, A. 2021. Okra in translation: Asylum seekers, food, and integration. *Language, Culture and Society* 3(1): 9–33.

Ciribuco, A. & O'Connor, A. 2022. Introduction: Translating the object, objects in translation: Theoretical and methodological notes on migration and materiality. *Translation and Interpreting Studies* 17(1): 1–13.

Classen, C. 1997. Foundations for an anthropology of the senses. *International Social Science Journal* 49(153): 401–12.

Classen, C., ed. 2005/2020. *The Book of Touch*. London: Routledge.

Classen, C. 2012. *The Deepest Sense: A Cultural History of Touch*. Champaign, IL: University of Illinois Press.

Classen, C. 2017. *The Museum of the Senses*. London: Bloomsbury.

Classen, C. & Howes, D. 2006. The museum as sensescape: Western sensibilities and indigenous artifacts. In E. Edwards, C. Gosden, & R. B. Phillips, eds., *Sensible Objects: Colonialism, Museums and Material Culture*. Oxford: Berg, 199–222.

Coldiron, A. E. B. 2023. Inside the kaleidoscope: Translation's challenge to critical concepts. *PMLA* 138(3): 419–35.

Cook, R. F. 1980. Translators and traducers: Some English versions of the 'Song of Roland', stanzas 83–85. *Olifant* 7(4): 327–42.

Coover, R. 1992. The end of books. *The New York Times* (21 June). https://archive.nytimes.com/www.nytimes.com/books/98/09/27/specials/coover-end.html.

Cowan, B., Laird, R., & McKeown, J. 2020. *Museum Objects, Health and Healing: The Exhibitions-Wellness Connection*. London: Routledge.

Cowley, S., ed. 2012. *Distributed Language*. Amsterdam: John Benjamins.

Danzker, J.-A. Birnie. 2012. Private/public in a time of lead. In M. Borja, ed., *Muntadas: Entre/Between*. Madrid: Museo Nacional Centro de Arte Reina Sofía, 59–63.

Dawkins, R. 2006. *The Selfish Gene*. (30th anniversary ed.). New York: Oxford University Press.

De Campos, H. 1982. Mephistofaustian transluciferation (Contribution to the semiotics of poetic translation). Trans. G. S. Wilder & H. de Campos. *Dispositio* 7(19–20): 181–87.

De Campos, H. 1983. Tradução, Ideologia e História. *Cadernos do MAM* 1: 58–64.

De Campos, H. 1992. Da tradução como criação e como crítica. In *Metalinguagem & Outras Metas*. Sao Paulo: Perspectiva, 31–48.

Deleuze, G. & Guattari, F. 1972/1984. *Anti-Oedipus: Capitalism and Schizophrenia*. Trans. R. Hurley, M. Seem, & H. R. Lane. New York: Penguin.

Deleuze, G. & Guattari, F. 1975/1986. *Kafka: Toward a Minor Literature*. Trans. Dana Polan. Minneapolis, MN: University of Minnesota Press.

Deleuze, G. & Guattari, F. 1980/1987. *A Thousand Plateaus: Capitalism and Schizophrenia*. Trans. B. Massumi. Minneapolis, MN: University of Minnesota Press.

Delisle, J., Lee-Jahnke, H., & Cormier, M. C., eds. 1999. *Translation Terminology*. Amsterdam: John Benjamins.

Desjardins, R. 2015. Food and translation on the table. *The Translator* 21(3): 257–70.

Downey, D., Kinane, I., & Parker, E., eds. 2018. *Landscapes of Liminality: Between Space and Place*. London: Rowman & Littlefield.

Emmerich, K. 2017. *Literary Translation and the Making of Originals*. London: Bloomsbury.

Flood, C. & M. R. Sloan. 2019. Introduction. In C. Flood & M. R. Sloan, eds., *Food: Bigger than the Plate*. London: Victoria and Albert Museum, 8–27.

Funkhouser, C. T. 2007. *Prehistoric Digital Poetry: An Archaeology of Forms, 1959–1995*. Tuscaloosa, AL: The University of Alabama Press.

Gadoua, M.-P. 2014. Making sense of touch. *The Senses & Society* 9(3): 323–41.

Genette, G. 1982/1997. *Palimpsests: Literature in the Second Degree*. Trans. C. Newman & C. Doubinsky. Lincoln, NE: University of Nebraska Press.

Genosko, G. 2002. *Felix Guattari: An Aberrant Introduction*. London: Continuum.

Glissant, É. 1997. *Traité du Tout-Monde*. Paris: Gallimard.

Glissant, É. 1990/1997. *Poetics of Relation*. Trans. Betsy Wing. Ann Arbor, MI: The University of Michigan Press.

Gómez, I. C. 2023. *Cannibal Translation: Literary Reciprocity in Contemporary Latin America*. Evanston, IL: Northwestern University Press.

Grass, D. 2023. *Translation as Creative-Critical Practice*. Cambridge: Cambridge University Press.

References

Grigar, D. & O'Sullivan, J., eds. 2021. *Electronic Literature as Digital Humanities*. London: Bloomsbury Academic.

Guo, Y., Peeta, S., Agrawal, S., & Benedyk, I. 2022. Impacts of Pokémon GO on route and mode choice decisions: Exploring the potential for integrating augmented reality, gamification, and social components in mobile apps to influence travel decisions. *Transportation* 49: 395–444.

Han, B.-C. 2022a. *Hyperculture: Culture and Globalization*. Trans. Daniel Steuer. Cambridge: Polity.

Han, B.-C. 2022b. *Non-Things: Upheaval in the Lifeworld*. Trans. Daniel Steuer. Cambridge: Polity.

Hawkins, M. R. 2018. Transmodalities and transnational encounters: Fostering critical cosmopolitan relations. *Applied Linguistics* 39(1): 55–77.

Hayles, N. K. 2002. *Writing Machines*. Cambridge, MA: The MIT Press.

Hayles, N. K. 2003. Translating media: Why we should rethink textuality. *The Yale Journal of Criticism* 16(2): 263–90.

Hayles, N. K. 2008. *Electronic Literature: New Horizons for the Literary*. Paris: University of Notre Dame.

Hayles, N. K. 2021. *Postprint: Books and Becoming Computational*. New York: Columbia University Press.

Hernández, R. 2010. Augusto de Campos: Traductor visible, traductor visual. *Hermēneus* 12: 147–60.

Hopkins, D. 2000. *After Modern Art 1945–2000*. Oxford: Oxford University Press.

Howes, D. & Classen, C. 2014. *Ways of Sensing: Understanding the Senses in Society*. London: Routledge.

Jackson, K. D. 2020. Transcreation without borders. In J. Corbett & T. Huang, eds., *The Translation and Transmission of Concrete Poetry*. London: Routledge, 97–111.

Jakobson, R. 1959/2012. On linguistic aspects of translation. In L. Venuti, ed., *The Translation Studies Reader* (3rd ed.). London: Routledge, 126–31.

Kress, G. & van Leeuwen, T. 2021. *Reading Images: The Grammar of Visual Design* (3rd ed.). London: Routledge.

Landow, G. P. 1992. *Hypertext: The Convergence of Contemporary Critical Theory and Technology*. Baltimore, MD: Johns Hopkins University Press.

Landow, G. P. 2006. *Hypertext 3.0: Critical Theory and New Media in an Era of Globalization*. Baltimore, MD: Johns Hopkins University Press.

Latour, B. 2005. *Reassembling the Social: An Introduction to Actor Network Theory*. Oxford: Oxford University Press.

Le Breton, D. 2006/2017. *Sensing the World: An Anthropology of Senses*. London: Bloomsbury Academic.

Leahy, H. R. 2012. *Museum Bodies: The Politics and Practices of Visiting and Viewing*. Hampshire: Ashgate.

Lee, T. K. 2014. Visuality and translation in contemporary Chinese literary art: Xu Bing's a book from the sky and a book from the ground. *Asia Pacific Translation and Intercultural Studies* 1(1): 43–62.

Lee, T. K. 2015. *Experimental Chinese literature: Translation, Technology, Poetics*. Leiden: Brill.

Lee, T. K. 2022. *Translation as Experimentalism*. Cambridge: Cambridge University Press.

Lee, T. K. 2023. Artificial intelligence and posthumanist translation: ChatGPT versus the translator. *Applied Linguistics Review* (ahead of print). https://doi.org/10.1515/applirev-2023-0122.

Li, W. 2018. Translanguaging as a practical theory of language. *Applied Linguistics* 39(1): 9–30.

Liu, A. 2011. The living word: Xu Bing and the art of Chan wordplay. In H. Tsao & R. T. Ames, eds., *Xu Bing and Contemporary Chinese Art: Cultural and Philosophical Reflections*. New York: SUNY Press, 117–46.

Lopez, T., ed. 2013. *The Text Festivals: Language Art and Material Poetry*. Plymouth: University of Plymouth Press.

Malmkjær, K. 2020. *Translation and Creativity*. London: Routledge.

Marais, Kobus. 2023. *Trajectories of Translation: The Thermodynamics of Semiosis*. London: Routledge.

Mellinger, C. 2024. Preface. In Mª Carmen África Vidal Claramonte, ed., *Translation and Repetition. Rewriting (Un)original Literature*. London: Routledge, vi–x.

Mersmann, B. 2019. Case studies of global transference: Language, media and culture translation in Xu Bing's writing-art. *Revista de Estudios Globales y Arte Contemporáneo* 6(1): 53–75.

Montagu, A. 1971. *Touching: The Human Significance of the Skin*. New York: Columbia University Press.

Morton, T. 2013. *Hyperobjects: Philosophy and Ecology after the End of the World*. Minneapolis, MN: University of Minnesota Press.

Narumi, T., Nishizaka, S., Kajinami, T., Tanikawa, T., & Hirose, M. 2011. Meta cookie+: An illusion-based gustatory display. In R. Shumaker, ed., *Virtual and Mixed Reality – New Trends. VMR 2011*. New York: Springer, 260–69.

O'Hagan, M. 2001. Hypertranslation. In N. Terashima & J. Tiffin, eds., *HyperReality: Paradigm for the Third Millenium*. London: Routledge, 99–109.

O'Sullivan, J. 2019. *Towards a Digital Poetics: Electronic Literature & Literary Games*. New York: Palgrave Macmillan.

Palumbo, G. 2009. *Key Terms in Translation Studies*. London: Continuum.

Pennycook, A. 2018. *Posthumanist Applied Linguistics*. London: Routledge.

Perloff, M. 2010. *Unoriginal Genius: Poetry by Other Means in the New Century*. Chicago, IL: University of Chicago Press.

Phillips, T. 2016. *A Humument: A Treated Victorian Novel*. London: Thames & Hudson.

Raley, R. 2009. *Tactical Media*. Minneapolis, MN: University of Minnesota Press.

Raley, R. 2016. Algorithmic translations. *CR: The New Centennial Review* 16(1): 115–37.

Rettberg, S. 2019. *Electronic Literature*. Cambridge: Polity.

Risku, H. & Rogl, R. 2021. Translation and situated, embodied, distributed, embedded and extended cognition. In F. Alves & A. L. Jakobsen, eds., *The Routledge Handbook of Translation and Cognition*. London: Routledge, 478–99.

Robert-Foley, L. 2024. *Experimental Translation: The Work of Translation in the Age of Algorithmic Production*. London: Goldsmiths Press.

Robinson, D. 2022. *The Experimental Translator*. New York: Springer.

Rodaway, P. 1994. *Sensuous Geographies: Body, Sense and Place*. London: Routledge.

Rosenberg, J. 2015. *Word Space Multiplicities, Openings, Andings*. Morgantown, WV: Center for Literary Computing.

Rothenberg, J. 2006. The anthology as a manifesto & as an epic including poetry, or the gradual making of poems for the millennium. *Revista Canaria de Estudios Ingleses* 52(April): 15–18.

Rothenberg, J. & Joris, P., eds. 1998. *Poems for the Millennium (Volume Two): From Postwar to Millennium*. Oakland, CA: University of California Press.

Salter, C. 2015. *Alien Agency: Experimental Encounters with Art in the Making*. Cambridge, MA: The MIT Press.

Sanders, J. 2016. *Adaptation and Appropriation* (2nd ed.). London: Routledge.

Scott, C. 2018. *The Work of Translation*. Cambridge: Cambridge University Press.

Scott, C. 2019. Synaesthesia and intersemiosis: Competing principles in literary translation. In M. Campbell & R. Vidal, eds., *Translating across Sensory and Linguistic Borders: Intersemiotic Journeys between Media*. New York: Palgrave Macmillan, 87–112.

Seddon, E. 2019. Exploring the social complexity of translation with assemblage thinking. In K. Marais & R. Meylaerts, eds., *Complexity Thinking in Translation Studies: Methodological Considerations*. London: Routledge, 104–27.

Seiça, A. 2021. Kinetic poetry. In D. Grigar & J. O'Sullivan, eds., *Electronic Literature as Digital Humanities*. London: Bloomsbury Academic, 173–202.

Shiratori, H. 白取春彦 2010. 超訳ニーチェの言葉 [Super-translating the words of Nietzsche]. Tokyo: Discover 21.

Shuttleworth, M. & Cowrie, M. 2014. *Dictionary of Translation Studies*. London: Routledge.

Silverman, R., ed. 2015. *Museum as Process: Translating Local and Global Knowledges*. London: Routledge.

Sleeper-Smith, S., ed. 2009. *Knowledge: Museums and Indigenous Perspectives*. Lincoln: University of Nebraska Press.

Soja, E. W. 1996. *Thirdspace: Journeys to Los Angeles and Other Real-and-Imagined Places*. Oxford: Blackwell.

Spitzer, S. 2012. Translator's preface. In A. Badiou, ed., *Plato's Republic: A Dialogue in Sixteen Chapters, with a Prologue and an Epilogue*. Trans. S. Spitzer. London: Polity, xxiv–xxviii.

Steffensen, S. V. 2015. Distributed language and dialogism: Notes on non-locality, sense-making and interactivity. *Language Sciences* 50: 105–119.

Sturge, K. 2014. The other on display: Translation in the ethnographic museum. In T. Hermans, ed., *Translating Others* (Vol. 2). London: Routledge, 431–40.

Tanasescu, R. 2024a. Literary translation on digital platforms: Intermedial and sonic perspectives. *The Translator* 30(3). Forthcoming special issue on Relation Thinking in Translation Studies.

Tanasescu, R. 2024b. Reimagining translation anthologies: A journey into non-linear computational assemblages. In C. Tanasescu, ed., *Literature and Computation: Platform Intermediality, Hermeneutic Modeling, and Analytical-Creative Approaches*. London: Routledge, 87–116.

Tanasescu, C. & Tanasescu, R. 2023. Complexity and analytical-creative approaches at scale: Iconicity, monstrosity, and #GraphPoem. In F. Armaselu & A. Fickers, eds., *Zoomland: Exploring Scale in Digital History and Humanities*. Berlin: De Gruyter, 237–60.

Thibault, P. J. 2011. First-order languaging dynamics and second-order language: The distributed language view. *Ecological Psychology* 23(3): 210–45.

Varis, P. & Blommaert, J. 2015. Conviviality and collectives on social media: Virality, memes, and new social structures. *Multilingual Margins* 2(1): 31–45.

Velasco, C. & Obrist, M. 2020. *Multisensory Experiences: Where the Senses Meet Technology*. Oxford: Oxford University Press.

Venuti, L. 2019. *Contra Instrumentalism: A Translation Polemic*. Lincoln, NE: University of Nebraska Press.

Vidal Claramonte, M. C. A. 2022. *Translation and Contemporary Art*. London: Routledge.

Vieira, E. R. P. 1994. A postmodern translational aesthetics in Brazil. In M. Snell-Hornby, F. Pöchhacker, & K. Kaindl, eds., *Translation Studies: An Interdiscipline*. Amsterdam: John Benjamins, 65–72.

Vieira, E. R. P. 1999. Liberating calibans: Readings of *Antropofagia* and Haroldo de Campos' poetics of transcreation. In S. Bassnett & H. Trivedi, eds., *Post-Colonial Translation: Theory and Practice*. London: Routledge, 95–113.

Washbourne, K. 2023. Against translation: An inquiry into the poetics of opposition and renewal. *Journal of Translation Studies* 7(2): 61–96.

Wolf, M. 2003. From anthropo-phagy to texto-phagy. *Todas as letras* 5: 117–28.

Zanelli, S. 2022. Chaosmosis: To chaotize order, to sieve chaos. *La Deleuziana – Online Journal of Philosophy* 15: 46–54.

Acknowledgements

We would like to thank John Cayley, Antoni Muntadas, and Jim Rosenberg for granting us permission to include images of their works in this manuscript. We are also indebted to a number of scholars whose comments and suggestions have enriched the final version of our work, among whom are Susan Bassnett and Raluca Tanasescu. Special thanks are extended to the AHRC-funded Experiential Translation Network (ETN), in particular to the two investigators Ricarda Vidal and Madeleine Campbell for their leadership on the project. Our participation in the ETN has significantly contributed to the articulation of many of the less conventional ideas on translation contained in this Element. We would also like to acknowledge *Traducción, ideología, cultura*, a research group based at the University of Salamanca to which the authors are affiliated. Last but not least, we are grateful to Kirsten Malmkjær, whose professionalism and expert guidance have greatly facilitated the publication of this work.

Cambridge Elements

Translation and Interpreting

The series is edited by Kirsten Malmkjær with Sabine Braun as associate editor for Elements focusing on Interpreting.

Kirsten Malmkjær
University of Leicester

Kirsten Malmkjær is Professor Emeritus of Translation Studies at the University of Leicester. She has taught Translation Studies at the universities of Birmingham, Cambridge, Middlesex and Leicester and has written extensively on aspects of both the theory and practice of the discipline. *Translation and Creativity* (London: Routledge) was published in 2020 and *The Cambridge Handbook of Translation*, which she edited, was published in 2022. She is preparing a volume entitled *Introducing Translation* for the Cambridge Introductions to Language and Linguistics series.

Editorial Board
Adriana Serban, *Université Paul Valéry*
Barbara Ahrens, *Technische Hochschule Köln*
Liu Min-Hua, *Hong Kong Baptist University*
Christine Ji, *The University of Sydney*
Jieun Lee, *Ewha Womans University*
Lorraine Leeson, *The University of Dublin*
Sara Laviosa, *Università Delgi Stuidi di Bari Aldo Moro*
Fabio Alves, *FALE-UFMG*
Moira Inghilleri, *University of Massachusetts Amherst*
Akiko Sakamoto, *University of Portsmouth*
Haidee Kotze, *Utrecht University*

About the Series
Elements in Translation and Interpreting present cutting edge studies on the theory, practice and pedagogy of translation and interpreting. The series also features work on machine learning and AI, and human-machine interaction, exploring how they relate to multilingual societies with varying communication and accessibility needs, as well as text-focused research.

Cambridge Elements

Translation and Interpreting

Elements in the Series

Translation as Experimentalism
Tong King Lee

Translation and Genre
B. J. Woodstein

On-Screen Language in Video Games
Mikołaj Deckert and Krzysztof W. Hejduk

Navigating the Web
Claire Y. Shih

The Graeco-Arabic Translation Movement
El-Hussein AY Aly

Interpreting as Translanguaging
Lili Han, Zhisheng (Edward) Wen and Alan James Runcieman

Creative Classical Translation
Paschalis Nikolaou

Translation as Creative–Critical Practice
Delphine Grass

Translation in Analytic Philosophy
Francesca Ervas

Towards Game Translation User Research
Mikołaj Deckert, Krzysztof W. Hejduk, and Miguel Á. Bernal-Merino

Hypertranslation
Mª Carmen África Vidal Claramonte and Tong King Lee

A full series listing is available at: www.cambridge.org/EITI